Blazor Fundamentals: Building Web Applications with Blazor and .NET 9

Adam Seebeck

unQbd

United States

Blazor Fundamentals: Building Web Applications with Blazor and .NET 9

Author: Adam Seebeck

Copy Editor: Samantha Seebeck

For permission to use material from this book, please contact:
https://www.unqbd.com/Contact
or email: PermissionRequest@unQbd.com

Hardcover ISBN: 978-1-954086-70-8
Paperback ISBN: 978-1-954086-69-2

Edition: 1.01

unQbd
581 N Park Ave #4201
Apopka, FL 32704
USA

Print Year: 2025

Unless otherwise noted, all items © unQbd.

unQbd (pronounced "un-cubed") is a modern book publishing and streaming platform. Readers can enjoy unlimited access to a growing library of books, including technical guides, fiction, and children's titles. All books can be read on any internet-connected device for one low annual price. Most titles are also available for purchase in print.

Discover unQbd

Read More. Learn More. Be Part of the Story.

unQbd is more than just books. It is your all-access pass to a world of stories, knowledge, and conversation. From gripping novels to expert tech guides, everything is available in one seamless experience on any device you choose.

Your free 7-day trial includes:

• Unlimited Reading and Listening
Enjoy full access to our entire library of books and audiobooks. Explore as much as you want, whenever you want.

• A Growing Collection
We regularly add new titles, exclusive releases, and interactive features to keep your experience fresh and exciting.

• Works on All Devices
No special apps required. Read or listen from your phone, tablet, or computer.

• Join the Conversation
Ask questions inside the book, connect directly with authors, and share your thoughts with other readers. unQbd is a reading experience built for community.

Start your free trial at unQbd.com
Scan the QR code below to get started.

Chapter 4: Razor Syntax and Data Binding

- Introduction to Razor Syntax
- Data Binding in Blazor
  - One-way Data Binding
  - Two-way Data Binding (@bind)
- Conditional Rendering (@if, @switch)
- Loops (@foreach)
- Full Example: Interactive Feedback Form
- Mini Quiz: Razor Syntax & Data Binding
- Activity: Build a Simple Survey Form

Chapter 5: State Management in Blazor

- Understanding State Management
- Component-Level State
- Application-Level State
- Cascading Parameters
- Full Example: Shared State with a Shopping Cart
- Mini Quiz: State Management
- Activity: Track Your Favorite Books

Chapter 6: Routing and Navigation

- Setting Up Routing
- Navigation Between Components
- Route Parameters
- Navigation Lifecycle Events
- Full Example: Route Parameters and Dynamic Navigation
- Mini Quiz: Routing and Navigation
- Activity: Build a Multi-Page Navigation System

Chapter 7: Forms and Validation

- Creating Blazor Forms
- Built-in Validation (Data Annotations)
- Custom Validation Logic
- Handling Form Submission
- Full Example: User Registration Form with Validation
- Mini Quiz: Forms and Validation
- Activity: Build a Newsletter Signup Form

Chapter 8: Dependency Injection in Blazor

- Understanding Dependency Injection
- Setting up Services
- Scoped, Singleton, and Transient Services
- Injecting Services into Components
- Full Example: Injecting and Using a Weather Forecast Service
- Mini Quiz: Dependency Injection
- Activity: Create and Inject a Greeting Service

Chapter 9: Communicating with APIs

- HTTP Client Configuration
- Fetching Data from REST APIs
- CRUD Operations with APIs
- Handling API Errors and Responses
- Full Example: Fetch and Display User Data from an API
- Mini Quiz: API Communication
- Activity: Create a Post Viewer from an API

Chapter 10: Security and Authentication in Blazor

- Authentication & Authorization Concepts
- Implementing Authentication
- Role-based Authorization
- Securing API Calls
- Full Example: Simulated Login with Conditional Access
- Mini Quiz: Security and Authentication
- Activity: Simulate a Role-Based Greeting

Chapter 11: JavaScript Interoperability (JS Interop)

- Why Use JavaScript with Blazor?
- JS Interop Basics
- Calling JavaScript from Blazor
- Calling Blazor from JavaScript
- Full Example: Scroll to Top with JavaScript
- Mini Quiz: JS Interoperability
- Activity: Display the Current Time Using JavaScript

Chapter 12: Advanced Component Concepts

- RenderFragment and Template Components
- Component References (@ref)
- EventCallback and Event Handling
- Error Handling in Components
- Full Example: Reusable Modal Dialog with RenderFragment and EventCallback
- Mini Quiz: Advanced Components
- Activity: Build a Reusable Notification Banner

Chapter 13: Styling and Responsive Design

- Applying CSS in Blazor Applications
- CSS Isolation in Components
- Using CSS Frameworks (Bootstrap, Tailwind)
- Responsive Design Best Practices
- Full Example: Themed Dashboard Panel with Responsive CSS
- Mini Quiz: Styling and Responsive Design
- Activity: Build a Styled, Responsive Profile Card

Chapter 14: Performance Optimization

- Measuring Performance in Blazor Apps
- Lazy Loading Components
- Optimizing Rendering Performance
- Data Virtualization Techniques
- Full Example: Virtualized Product List with Optimized Rendering
- Mini Quiz: Performance Optimization
- Activity: Optimizing Your Application

Chapter 15: Testing Blazor Components

- Introduction to Testing in Blazor
- Setting Up bUnit
- Writing Your First Component Test
- Testing Component Lifecycle and Rendering
- Mocking Dependencies and Services
- Advanced bUnit Testing Techniques
- Full Example: Writing and Running a bUnit Test for a Component
- Mini Quiz: Testing Blazor Components
- Activity: Build a Full Test Suite for a Real Component

- Mini Quiz: Error Logging and Monitoring
- Activity: Add Logging and Monitoring

Chapter 20: Deployment and Hosting

- Hosting Options (Azure, IIS, Static Hosting)
- Deploying Blazor Server Applications
- Deploying Blazor WebAssembly Applications
- Continuous Integration and Delivery (CI/CD)
- Mini Quiz: Deployment and Hosting
- Activity: Publish Your Blazor App to GitHub Pages

Final Thought and Next Steps

- Next Steps in Your Blazor Journey
- Resources for Further Learning
- Getting Involved in the Community
- Encouragement and Closing Words

Welcome to **Blazor Fundamentals: Building Web Applications with Blazor and .NET**, a hands-on guide crafted specifically to teach you how to build dynamic, modern web applications using Microsoft's innovative Blazor framework.

Written by Adam Seebeck, a seasoned higher education instructor and experienced developer, this book is designed to be more than just reading material. It's structured as an interactive course that takes you on a journey through practical, engaging examples, quizzes, and exercises, ensuring you master the concepts thoroughly.

Whether you are a seasoned .NET developer looking to expand your skillset into the web development domain or a complete newcomer eager to understand the power of Blazor, you'll find the approach in this book both accessible and robust.

Who Should Read This Book?

This book is ideal for anyone who:

- Has experience with C# or .NET and wants to leverage those skills to build powerful web applications.

- Is completely new to web development but familiar with basic programming concepts and eager to learn through structured guidance.

- Wishes to understand and master modern web development practices using Microsoft's technologies.

- Wants practical experience building interactive, scalable applications that run seamlessly across browsers and devices.

What You'll Learn

By the end of this book, you will be able to:

- Create interactive, real-world web applications entirely with C#.

- Understand and implement component-based architectures to build reusable and maintainable web UIs.

- Manage state effectively to ensure responsive and reliable user experiences.

- Integrate your applications with RESTful APIs and third-party services.

- Secure your Blazor applications using modern authentication and authorization techniques.

- Optimize performance and deploy robust Blazor applications to production environments confidently.

Unique Teaching Techniques in this Book

This book employs the following teaching methods to enhance your learning experience:

Quick Reference Essentials

Each topic begins with a clear, concise explanation accompanied by practical code snippets, quickly orienting you to the key concepts.

Full Examples

Real-world scenarios help deepen your understanding, demonstrating clearly how concepts are used in actual Blazor applications.

Step-by-Step Walkthroughs

Detailed walkthroughs guide you from start to finish, providing all the information needed to build complete, fully functional Blazor apps.

Interactive Activities

Hands-on exercises let you immediately apply your newfound knowledge, reinforcing the material as you progress.

Mini Quizzes

Brief quizzes at the end of major sections provide checkpoints for understanding, ensuring you remain confident as you move forward.

How to Get the Most from this Book

- **Follow Sequentially:**
  For the most comprehensive learning experience, it's recommended you proceed chapter-by-chapter. Each section builds logically upon the previous, progressively increasing in complexity.

- **Engage Actively:**
  Take the time to complete the activities and quizzes. This interactive approach significantly boosts comprehension and retention.

- **Reference Regularly:**
  Use this book as an ongoing resource to quickly refresh your knowledge of key Blazor concepts, code patterns, and best practices.

What You Need

To effectively work through this book, you'll need:

- Visual Studio 2022 or later (Community Edition is free and recommended).

- Basic familiarity with C# programming.

- Enthusiasm and curiosity about modern web development techniques.

Additional Resources

Throughout the book, you will find links and references to official Microsoft documentation, community forums, and recommended further reading to support your learning.

Let's Begin!

You're about to embark on a rewarding journey into modern web development using Blazor. As we dive into each chapter, remember to experiment, ask questions, and challenge yourself. Let's get started building powerful, interactive web applications!

CHAPTER 1: INTRODUCTION TO BLAZOR

Blazor is a modern web framework from Microsoft that lets you build rich, interactive web apps using **C# and Razor syntax**, without relying heavily on JavaScript. In this chapter, you'll learn what makes Blazor unique, how it works, and why it's changing how developers approach web development.

By the end of this chapter, you will:

- Understand the purpose and benefits of Blazor

- Distinguish between Blazor Server and Blazor WebAssembly (WASM)

- Recognize key improvements introduced in .NET 9

- See how Blazor compares to traditional frontend frameworks like Angular and React

What is Blazor?

Blazor allows developers to create web applications using **C# instead of JavaScript**. It uses a component-based architecture that supports reusability and separation of concerns—concepts familiar to any .NET developer. With Blazor, you can write both client-side and server-side logic in a single language and platform, simplifying the development process and reducing the need to switch between tools or ecosystems.

Why Choose Blazor?

Blazor offers several advantages that make it appealing to both individual developers and teams:

Unified Development

Write both client and server code in C#, eliminating the need for extensive JavaScript knowledge or complex frontend build tooling.

Component-Based Architecture

Break your UI into reusable components for better organization, easier maintenance, and faster development.

Productivity and Tooling

Blazor integrates with the entire .NET ecosystem—so you can reuse libraries, leverage Visual Studio tooling, and work with familiar patterns like dependency injection and strong typing.

Performance

Blazor Server delivers fast initial loads with real-time UI updates using SignalR. Blazor WebAssembly runs directly in the browser for near-native speed.

Blazor Hosting Models

Blazor supports three primary hosting models, each suited for different use cases:

Blazor Server

Runs on the server. The client connects via SignalR for UI updates.

- ☑ Fast load times, small downloads

- ☑ Easy access to server resources

- ⚠ Requires constant internet connection

- ⚠ Latency can impact responsiveness

Blazor WebAssembly (WASM)

Runs entirely in the browser using WebAssembly.

- ☑ Works offline, good for PWAs

- ☑ Can be deployed as static files

- ⚠ Larger initial download

- ⚠ WebAssembly limitations apply

Blazor Hybrid (.NET MAUI)

Combines Blazor with native desktop or mobile apps via .NET MAUI.

- ☑ True cross-platform (Windows, macOS, Android, iOS)

- ☑ Native-like speed and experience

- ⚠ More complex due to native integration requirements

What's New in Blazor with .NET 9?

Blazor continues to evolve. Here are a few standout features added in .NET 9:

- Faster load times and better memory usage

- Improved built-in authentication tools

- Enhanced CSS isolation for cleaner component styling

- Better debugging in Visual Studio, especially with WebAssembly

Blazor Compared to Other Frontend Frameworks

When compared to popular JavaScript frameworks such as Angular, React, and Vue, Blazor stands out due to its unique strengths:

Feature	Blazor	Angular / React / Vue
Language Consistency	C# (.NET)	JavaScript / TypeScript
Performance	Excellent (WebAssembly)	Excellent (Varies by Framework)
Component Architecture	Yes	Yes
Learning Curve	Lower for .NET developers	Higher for .NET developers
Integration	Seamless with .NET	More effort required

Blazor's primary appeal is the ease of adopting modern web development practices without the need to deeply learn and manage separate frontend and backend technologies.

1. **Which programming language does Blazor primarily use for building web applications?**

   o   A) JavaScript

   o   B) TypeScript

   o   C) C#

   o   D) HTML5

2. **Which Blazor hosting model requires a constant connection to the server?**

   o   A) Blazor WebAssembly

   o   B) Blazor Server

   o   C) Blazor Hybrid

3. **What technology enables Blazor WebAssembly apps to run in the browser?**

   o   A) JavaScript

   o   B) TypeScript

   o   C) WebAssembly

   o   D) SignalR

4. **Which Blazor model is best for offline application scenarios?**

   o   A) Blazor WebAssembly

   o   B) Blazor Server

Answers:

1. C
2. B
3. C
4. A

In this chapter, you'll set up your development environment, install and configure essential tools, and create your first Blazor Web App using the latest unified hosting model introduced in .NET 8 and improved in .NET 9.

By the end of this chapter, you will:

- Install Visual Studio 2022 or later

- Configure Visual Studio specifically for Blazor development

- Create your first Blazor Web App using the new template

- Understand the structure of a Blazor project

- Learn how to run and debug your Blazor application

Visual Studio Installation

Step-by-Step Walkthrough:

1. Go to the official Visual Studio download page: https://visualstudio.microsoft.com/downloads/.

2. Select the **Community Edition** (free and recommended).

3. Run the downloaded installer and follow the on-screen instructions.

4. During installation, select the **ASP.NET and web development** workload to ensure Blazor support.

Configuring Visual Studio for Blazor

After installation, ensure Visual Studio is properly configured:

1. Open Visual Studio.

2. Navigate to **Tools > Get Tools and Features** if additional workloads or components are needed.

3. Confirm that the **ASP.NET and web development** workload is installed.

Creating Your First Blazor Web App

.NET 9 introduces a new default Blazor project template called **Blazor Web App**. This unified template allows you to mix server-side and client-side interactivity within a single project, eliminating the need to choose between Blazor Server or Blazor WebAssembly up front.

Step-by-Step Walkthrough:

1. Launch Visual Studio and select **Create a new project**.

2. In the project templates, search for "Blazor Web App".

3. Choose **Blazor Web App** from the list.

4. Name your project, select a save location, and click **Next**.

5. Ensure **.NET 9** is selected as the Framework.

6. Choose the desired interactive render mode (e.g., Server for this book's examples).

7. Leave authentication as "None" and click **Create**.

Exploring Blazor Project Structure

After creating your Blazor Web App project in .NET 9, take a moment to understand the layout and purpose of each folder and file. This structure is designed for clarity, modularity, and performance.

- **wwwroot:** This is the **web root** of your application. It holds static assets that are served directly to the browser, such as CSS files, JavaScript libraries, fonts, and images. Files in this folder are publicly accessible.
- **Components:** This folder contains **reusable UI components**, grouped by function and purpose. It is a key part of organizing a Blazor Web App.
  - **Pages:** Contains *.razor* files that represent navigable pages in your app. Each file typically includes a *@page* directive and represents a routable view, such as */index* or */login*.

- ○ **Layout:** Holds shared layout components, such as *MainLayout.razor*, *Header.razor*, or *NavMenu.razor*. These are used to define consistent structure across pages, such as headers, navigation bars, and footers.
- ○ **App.razor:** Serves as the **root component** for your Blazor application. It contains the *Router* and layout definition, which handle routing logic and determine which components to display based on the current URL.
- ○ **Routes.razor:** Introduced in .NET 9, this file **centralizes route configuration** for your app. You can define available routes and associate them with their corresponding components, making routing easier to manage in large apps.
- **Program.cs:** This is the **entry point** of your Blazor Web App. It sets up services, configures the rendering mode (e.g., Server or WebAssembly), and registers root components. You will often modify this file to add services to the dependency injection container.

Running and Debugging Blazor Applications

Getting your Blazor Web App up and running is simple with Visual Studio. Here's how to launch and debug your application:

1. **Start the App**
   Press **F5** or click the green **Run** button to build and launch your application.

2. **View in Browser**
   Your default web browser will open automatically, displaying your Blazor app.

3. **Set Breakpoints for Debugging**
   You can set breakpoints in your Razor files or C# classes:

   - ○ Click in the margin next to a line number to place a breakpoint.

   - ○ When the application hits a breakpoint, Visual Studio will pause execution.

   - ○ You can then inspect variables, step through code, and evaluate the current application state.

4. **Stop the App**
   To end the running session, click the **red square** (Stop button) in the toolbar.

Congratulations. You have just run and debugged your first Blazor application.

FULL EXAMPLE: HELLO FROM BLAZOR

Before we dive into building components from scratch, let's start by editing the page that comes with your new Blazor Web App: *Home.razor*.

When you run the app for the first time, you will see the text **"Hello, world!"** on the home page. That message comes from the *Home.razor* file, located in the *Components/Pages* folder.

Step 1: Open Home.razor

In **Solution Explorer**, navigate to:

```
Components > Pages > Home.razor
```

Replace the contents of the file with the following:

```
<h3>Hello, @UserName!</h3>
<p>Welcome to your Blazor Web App.</p>

@code {
    private string UserName = "Developer";
}
```

Step 2: Save and Run the App

Press **F5** or click the **Run** button in Visual Studio. Your browser will refresh and now display a personalized welcome message:
"Hello, Developer!"

In the next chapter, you'll learn what a **component** is, how it works, and how to build your own from scratch. For now, you've taken your first step toward customizing your Blazor application.

MINI QUIZ: DEVELOPMENT ENVIRONMENT

1. **Which Visual Studio workload must be selected for Blazor development?**

   o   A) Python Development

   o   B) ASP.NET and web development

   o   C) Desktop Development with C++

   o   D) Mobile Development

2. **What is the entry point for configuring services and middleware in a Blazor application?**

   o   A) Index.razor

   o   B) App.razor

   o   C) Program.cs

   o   D) MainLayout.razor

3. **Which directory contains Razor pages navigable by URL?**

   o   A) Shared

   o   B) Pages

   o   C) wwwroot

   o   D) Components

Answers:

1. B
2. C
3. B

Blazor applications are built using **components**, which serve as the fundamental units of UI and logic. Components are reusable, encapsulated pieces of Razor code that define part of the user interface.

In this chapter, you will:

- Understand what Blazor components are and how they work

- Create and render your own components

- Pass data into components using parameters

- Explore component lifecycle methods

What Are Components?

A **component** in Blazor is a self-contained block of UI with its own rendering logic and optional interactivity. Components are written using Razor syntax, a combination of HTML and C#.

Each *.razor* file represents a component. Components can be used to structure the layout of a page, reuse common UI elements, and encapsulate behavior.

Example:

```
<!-- WelcomeMessage.razor -->
<h3>Welcome to Blazor!</h3>
```

This simple component renders a heading. You can now use <WelcomeMessage /> in other Razor files.

Creating and Using Components

Step-by-Step Walkthrough:

1. Right-click the Components folder in your project.

2. Select **Add > Razor Component**.

3. Name the component *Greeting.razor*.

4. Add the following markup:

```
<h4>Hello from a custom component!</h4>
```

5. Open *Pages/Home.razor* and add the component:

```
<Greeting />
```

6. Run the app. You'll see the greeting rendered on the homepage.

Passing Parameters

Components can accept **parameters** to become more dynamic.

Example: Personalized Greeting

```
<!-- Greeting.razor -->
<h4>Hello, @Name!</h4>

@code {
    [Parameter]
    public string Name { get; set; }
}
```

Now update the usage:

```
<Greeting Name="Adam" />
```

Component Lifecycle

Blazor components follow a lifecycle that includes several events you can use to handle setup, data loading, updates, and cleanup. These lifecycle methods can be overridden to perform specific tasks at different stages of a component's life.

Common Lifecycle Methods

- **OnInitialized / OnInitializedAsync**
  Called once when the component is initialized. Ideal for setting up default values or making initial API calls.

- **OnParametersSet / OnParametersSetAsync**
  Called each time component parameters are set or updated. Useful when a component depends on parameter values passed from a parent.

- **OnAfterRender / OnAfterRenderAsync**
  Called after the component has rendered. Useful for interacting with the DOM or triggering JavaScript interop.

Example:

```
@code {
    protected override void OnInitialized()
    {
        Console.WriteLine("Component initialized.");
    }
}
```

What You Learned

This chapter introduced the core lifecycle methods to help you manage setup and behavior within your components. In **Chapter 12**, you will go deeper with advanced techniques including *@ref*, *RenderFragment*, and structured error handling for more control over rendering and interaction.

You have now created and rendered components, passed data using parameters, and explored the component lifecycle. These are essential building blocks for developing rich, reusable user interfaces in Blazor.

FULL EXAMPLE: REUSABLE TOGGLE MESSAGE COMPONENT

This example introduces a simple but useful component that teaches key Blazor concepts: parameters, internal state, conditional rendering, and event handling. You'll build a *ToggleMessage* component that lets users reveal or hide a message by clicking a button.

Step 1: Create *ToggleMessage.razor*

```
<div>
    <p>@(showMessage ? Message : HiddenText)</p>
    <button @onclick="Toggle">Toggle Message</button>
</div>

@code {
    [Parameter] public string Message { get; set; } = "You found the
secret!";
    [Parameter] public string HiddenText { get; set; } = "Click to
reveal the message.";

    private bool showMessage = false;

    private void Toggle()
    {
        showMessage = !showMessage;
    }
}
```

This component accepts two parameters (*Message* and *HiddenText*) and switches between them when the button is clicked. The internal *showMessage* flag keeps track of the toggle state.

Step 2: Use *ToggleMessage* in *Home.razor* or any parent component

Make sure your page supports interactive components. Add this line at the top of your *Home.razor* file:

```
@rendermode InteractiveServer
```

Then add your component instances below:

```
<h3>Try the Toggle Message</h3>

<ToggleMessage Message="Hello from your first component!"
              HiddenText="Click the button to see the message." />

<ToggleMessage Message="Blazor is awesome!"
              HiddenText="Want to know why?" />
```

Key Concepts

- **Parameters** let you reuse the same component with different text.

- **Private state** (*showMessage*) controls dynamic behavior inside the component.

- **Event handling** with *@onclick* updates the UI instantly when the user clicks the button.

- The *@rendermode InteractiveServer* directive is required for user interaction to work in .NET 9 Blazor Web Apps.

MINI QUIZ: COMPONENTS FUNDAMENTALS

1. **What is the file extension used for a Blazor component?**

    o   A) .cshtml

    o   B) .html

    o   C) .razor

    o   D) .jsx

2. **How do you pass a value to a component?**

    o   A) Via global variables

    o   B) Using ViewBag

    o   C) Using [Parameter]

    o   D) With @using

3. **Which method is used to run code when a component is initialized?**

    o   A) Start()

    o   B) InitializeComponent()

    o   C) OnInitialized()

    o   D) ComponentLoad()

Answers:

1. C
2. C
3. C

ACTIVITY: BUILD AND REUSE A COMPONENT

Objective: Create a simple reusable component and display it on the homepage.

Steps:

- Create a Razor component called *TipCard.razor* in the *Components* folder.

- Add the following markup:

```
<div class="tip-box">
    <strong>Tip:</strong> @Message
</div>

@code {
    [Parameter] public string Message { get; set; }
}
```

- Add the following CSS to *wwwroot/app.css*:

```
.tip-box {
    border: 1px solid #ccc;
    padding: 10px;
    background-color: #f9f9f9;
    margin-top: 10px;
}
```

- Open *Pages/Home.razor* and add this line:

```
<TipCard Message="Use components to keep your app modular and clean!" />
```

☑ Bonus Challenge:

Add a second parameter *Color* and apply it to the text color using inline styles.

CHAPTER 4: RAZOR SYNTAX AND DATA BINDING

In this chapter, you'll explore the Razor syntax used in Blazor applications and learn how to bind data dynamically.

By the end of this chapter, you'll be able to:

- Understand and use Razor syntax effectively

- Implement one-way and two-way data binding

- Use conditional rendering and loops in your UI

Introduction to Razor Syntax

Razor is a markup syntax for embedding server-side C# logic within HTML markup. Razor makes building dynamic web pages intuitive by combining HTML with inline C# logic.

Basic Razor Syntax Example:

```
<h3>@("Hello, " + userName + "!")</h3>

@code {
    string userName = "Adam";
}
```

Data Binding in Blazor

Blazor supports two primary data binding approaches:

One-way Data Binding

One-way binding pushes data from the component's logic to the UI.

Example:

```
<p>Current count: @currentCount</p>

@code {
    int currentCount = 5;
}
```

Two-way Data Binding

Two-way binding keeps your UI and component state in sync. When the user types into an input field, the value in your component is automatically updated, and any changes to the component value are reflected in the UI.

Example:

```
<input @bind="userInput" @bind:event="oninput" placeholder="Enter
text here" />
<p>You typed: @userInput</p>

@code {
    string userInput = string.Empty;
}
```

Note: The *@bind:event="oninput"* part tells Blazor to update the value as the user types. Without it, the value only updates when the input loses focus or you press enter.

Working with Radio Buttons

Blazor supports radio buttons using the *InputRadioGroup* and *InputRadio* components.

Example:

```
<InputRadioGroup @bind-Value="favoriteColor">
    <InputRadio Value="Red" /> Red
    <InputRadio Value="Blue" /> Blue
</InputRadioGroup>

<p>You selected: @favoriteColor</p>

@code {
    private string favoriteColor;
}
```

Conditional Rendering

Razor provides control structures like *@if* and *@switch* for conditional rendering.

Using @if:

```
@if (isLoggedIn)
{
    <p>Welcome back!</p>
}
else
{
    <p>Please log in.</p>
}

@code {
    bool isLoggedIn = true;
}
```

Loops (@foreach)

Loops allow rendering of repetitive elements dynamically.

Example:

```
<ul>
@foreach (var fruit in fruits)
{
    <li>@fruit</li>
}
</ul>

@code {
    string[] fruits = { "Apple", "Banana", "Cherry" };
}
```

FULL EXAMPLE : INTERACTIVE FEEDBACK FORM

This form shows how to use two-way data binding, validation, and conditional rendering. You'll let users enter their name and a short message and display a thank-you note after submission.

FeedbackForm.razor

```razor
@page "/feedback"
@using System.ComponentModel.DataAnnotations

<h3>Feedback</h3>

@if (!submitted)
{
    <EditForm Model="@feedback" OnValidSubmit="HandleSubmit"
FormName="feedbackForm">
        <DataAnnotationsValidator />
        <ValidationSummary />

        <InputText @bind-Value="feedback.Name" placeholder="Your name" />
        <ValidationMessage For="@(() => feedback.Name)" />

        <br />

        <InputTextArea @bind-Value="feedback.Message" placeholder="Your
message" />
        <ValidationMessage For="@(() => feedback.Message)" />

        <br />

        <button type="submit">Send</button>
    </EditForm>
}
else
{
    <p>Thanks, @feedback.Name! You wrote:</p>
    <blockquote>@feedback.Message</blockquote>
}

@code {
    private Feedback feedback = new();
    private bool submitted = false;

    private void HandleSubmit() => submitted = true;
```

```
public class Feedback
{
    [Required] public string Name { get; set; }
    [Required] public string Message { get; set; }
}
}
```

MINI QUIZ: RAZOR SYNTAX & DATA BINDING

1. Which directive is used for two-way data binding in Blazor?

    o A) @bind

    o B) @model

    o C) @data

    o D) @sync

2. What Razor syntax would you use for conditional rendering?

    o A) <% if %>

    o B) @if

    o C) {% if %}

    o D) #if

3. How do you iterate through a collection in Razor?

    o A) @repeat

    o B) @forEach

    o C) @loop

    o D) @foreach

Answers:

1. A
2. B
3. D

ACTIVITY: BUILD A SIMPLE SURVEY FORM

Objective: Practice Razor syntax, two-way binding, and conditional rendering by building a user survey component.

Steps:

- Create a new Razor component called SurveyForm.razor.

- Ask the question: *"Do you enjoy learning Blazor?"*

- Use two radio buttons labeled **Yes** and **No**, and bind them to a string variable named response.

- Use *@if* statements to conditionally show:

  - *"That's great to hear!"* if Yes is selected

  - *"Thanks for your honesty!"* if No is selected

☑ Bonus Challenge:

Instead of text responses, display a custom emoji or icon next to each message based on the user's answer.

Managing state effectively is crucial to creating responsive, robust, and scalable Blazor applications. State management involves handling data across different components, ensuring consistency and persistence of data throughout user interactions.

In this chapter, you will:

- Learn the concept of state management

- Manage component-level and application-level state

- Implement cascading parameters for shared state

Understanding State Management

State management refers to techniques for maintaining data across various parts of your application. Efficient state management ensures that the UI accurately reflects the current application state at all times.

In Blazor, state can be managed at two primary levels:

- **Component-level state:** Local to a single component.

- **Application-level state:** Shared across multiple components.

Component-Level State

Component-level state is data relevant only within a single component.

Example:

```
<button @onclick="Increment">Clicked @clickCount times</button>

@code {
    private int clickCount = 0;

    void Increment()
    {
        clickCount++;
    }
}
```

Here, *clickCount* is a component-level state maintained within the component itself.

Application-Level State

Application-level state is data shared across multiple components. A common approach is to use services to handle shared data.

Step-by-Step Example: Shared State with a Service

To share state across multiple components, you can create a service using a standard C# class.

How to Create a Class File

To add a new service file:

1. In **Solution Explorer**, right-click on the folder Components.

2. Choose **Add > Class**.

3. Name the file **CounterService.cs**, then click **Add**.

You'll write plain C# code in this file to manage shared logic or state.

1. Create a Service:

```
// CounterService.cs
public class CounterService
{
    public int Count { get; private set; } = 0;

    public void Increment() => Count++;
}
```

2. Register the Service:

Open *Program.cs* and add the following line **after** *var builder =*
WebApplication.CreateBuilder(args); and **before** *builder.Build();*:

```
builder.Services.AddScoped<CounterService>();
```

Your file will look like this:

```
var builder = WebApplication.CreateBuilder(args);

builder.Services.AddScoped<CounterService>(); // Register service

builder.Services.AddRazorComponents()
    .AddInteractiveServerComponents();

var app = builder.Build();
```

3. Use the Service in Components:

```
@inject CounterService counterService

<button @onclick="Increment">Clicked @counterService.Count
times</button>

@code {
    void Increment()
    {
        counterService.Increment();
    }
}
```

Now, multiple components can share and update the same *CounterService* instance. For example, if you click the button three times on one page, then navigate to another page that also uses this service, the count will still show **3**.

Cascading Parameters

Cascading parameters allow you to pass values down through a component hierarchy without manually passing them through every level.

Step 1: Create *ThemeChild.razor*

```
<p style="color:@ThemeColor">This text inherits the theme color.</p>

@code {
    [CascadingParameter] public string ThemeColor { get; set; }
}
```

This child component receives the value of *ThemeColor* from its parent, without requiring an explicit parameter.

Step 2: Use it in a Parent Component

```
<CascadingValue Value="themeColor">
    <ThemeChild />
</CascadingValue>

@code {
    string themeColor = "blue";
}
```

The parent wraps the child in a *CascadingValue* and supplies the value. The child can now access *ThemeColor* directly.

Cascading parameters are especially useful when you want to share data across many components, such as theme settings, user context, or app configuration. You'll see this pattern again later in the book when we work with layout components and dependency injection.

If this feels a little advanced, that's okay. The more you build with Blazor, the more natural it will become.

FULL EXAMPLE: SHARED STATE WITH A SHOPPING CART

This example demonstrates both component-level and application-level state using a service injected into multiple components.

CartService.cs

```
public class CartService
{
    public List<string> Items { get; } = new();

    public event Action CartUpdated;

    public void AddItem(string item)
    {
        Items.Add(item);
        CartUpdated?.Invoke();
    }

    public void RemoveItem(string item)
    {
        Items.Remove(item);
        CartUpdated?.Invoke();
    }

    public void ClearCart()
    {
        Items.Clear();
        CartUpdated?.Invoke();
    }
}
```

Register the Service in *Program.cs*

Add this line after *WebApplication.CreateBuilder(args);* and before *builder.Build();*

```
builder.Services.AddScoped<CartService>();
```

ProductList.razor

```
@inject CartService CartService

<h3>Available Products</h3>

<button class="btn btn-outline-primary" @onclick='() =>
CartService.AddItem("Apple")'>Add Apple</button>
<button class="btn btn-outline-primary" @onclick='() =>
CartService.AddItem("Banana")'>Add Banana</button>
<button class="btn btn-outline-primary" @onclick='() =>
CartService.AddItem("Orange")'>Add Orange</button>
```

Cart.razor

```
@inject CartService CartService

<h3>Your Shopping Cart</h3>

@if (CartService.Items.Count == 0)
{
    <p>Your cart is empty.</p>
}
else
{
    <ul>
        @foreach (var item in CartService.Items)
        {
            <li>
                @item
                <button class="btn btn-sm btn-danger" @onclick='() =>
CartService.RemoveItem(item)'>Remove</button>
            </li>
        }
    </ul>

    <button class="btn btn-warning"
@onclick="CartService.ClearCart">Clear Cart</button>
}

@code {
    protected override void OnInitialized()
    {
        CartService.CartUpdated += Refresh;
    }
```

```csharp
    private void Refresh() => InvokeAsync(StateHasChanged);

    public void Dispose()
    {
        CartService.CartUpdated -= Refresh;
    }
}
```

Create a Page to Use the Components (e.g., *CartPage.razor*)

```razor
@rendermode InteractiveServer
@page "/shop"

<h2>Simple Shopping Experience</h2>

<ProductList />
<Cart />
```

MINI QUIZ: STATE MANAGEMENT

1. Which type of state is local to a single component?

    o   A) Application-level state

    o   B) Component-level state

    o   C) Global state

    o   D) Session state

2. What Blazor feature easily shares data down a component hierarchy?

    o   A) Data binding

    o   B) Cascading parameters

    o   C) Dependency Injection

    o   D) Razor components

3. How do you typically share state across multiple components?

    o   A) Local variables

    o   B) Scoped services

    o   C) Static fields

    o   D) Direct DOM manipulation

Answers:

1. B
2. B
3. B

ACTIVITY: TRACK YOUR FAVORITE BOOKS

Objective: Use application-level state to create a service that shares data between components.

Steps:

- Create a new service called *FavoritesService* with a *List<string>* and methods *AddBook(string)* and *RemoveBook(string)*.

- Register the service as scoped in *Program.cs*.

- Create two Razor components:

    1. *BookSelector.razor* – Add buttons to add "1984", "Pride and Prejudice", and "Dune"

    2. *FavoriteBooks.razor* – List the selected books and show a "Remove" button next to each

- Use *@inject* to access the shared service in both components.

- Display both components in a parent page (e.g. *FavoritesPage.razor*)

☑ Bonus Challenge:

Add a "Clear All" button in *FavoriteBooks.razor* to remove all books from the list at once.

Routing is how users move between different views or pages in your Blazor application. It determines which component should be rendered when a specific URL is requested.

In this chapter, you will:

- Understand how routing works in Blazor

- Define and navigate between routes

- Pass route parameters

- Use navigation lifecycle events

Understanding Routing in Blazor

Blazor uses the *@page* directive to associate a component with a specific URL. This directive must be placed at the top of a *.razor* file.

Example:

```
@page "/about"

<h3>About Page</h3>
<p>This page is routed to /about</p>
```

When the user navigates to */about*, this component is rendered.

Defining Routes

You define a route by adding *@page "/your-path"* to the top of a Razor component. Each route must start with a / and be unique across your app.

Example:

```
@page "/contact"
<h3>Contact Page</h3>
```

How Routing Works in .NET 9 Blazor Web Apps

In .NET 9, routing is configured using **two files**:

App.razor **(root-level configuration)**

```
<Router AppAssembly="@typeof(App).Assembly">
    <Routes />
</Router>
```

This tells Blazor to look for route definitions in the *Routes.razor* file.

Routes.razor **(route layout and fallback)**

```
<Found Context="routeData">
    <RouteView RouteData="@routeData"
DefaultLayout="typeof(MainLayout)" />
</Found>
<NotFound>
    <LayoutView Layout="typeof(MainLayout)">
        <p>Sorry, there's nothing at this address.</p>
    </LayoutView>
</NotFound>
```

You typically won't need to change these unless you're modifying layouts or advanced routing behavior.

Navigating Between Pages

Use the *NavLink* component for navigation between internal pages. It automatically applies an *active* CSS class to the currently selected link.

Example:

```
<NavLink href="/about" class="nav-link" activeClass="active">About</NavLink>
```

To navigate programmatically, inject the *NavigationManager* service:

```
@inject NavigationManager Navigation

<button @onclick="GoToHome">Go Home</button>

@code {
    void GoToHome()
    {
        Navigation.NavigateTo("/");
    }
}
```

Route Parameters

Blazor supports passing parameters directly in the URL using placeholders.

Example:

```
@page "/user/{username}"

<h3>Hello, @username!</h3>

@code {
    [Parameter]
    public string username { get; set; }
}
```

Optional Parameters

You can make parameters optional by defining multiple routes:

```
@page "/greet"
@page "/greet/{name}"

<h3>Hello, @name!</h3>

@code {
    [Parameter]
    public string name { get; set; } = "Guest";
}
```

Now both */greet* and */greet/Sam* will work.

FULL EXAMPLE: ROUTE PARAMETERS AND DYNAMIC NAVIGATION

This example demonstrates how to define multiple routes, use parameters in the URL, and navigate programmatically within a Blazor application.

UserPage.razor

```razor
@page "/user/{username}"
@inject NavigationManager Navigation

<h3>Hello, @username!</h3>

@if (!string.IsNullOrEmpty(username))
{
    <button class="btn btn-primary" @onclick="GoHome">Go Home</button>
}

@code {
    [Parameter]
    public string username { get; set; }

    void GoHome()
    {
        Navigation.NavigateTo("/");
    }
}
```

This page greets the user by their name (passed in the URL) and offers a button to navigate back to the home page.

Home.razor

```razor
@page "/"

<h3>Welcome to the Home Page</h3>

<NavLink class="nav-link" href="/user/Alice">Greet Alice</NavLink>
<NavLink class="nav-link" href="/user/Bob">Greet Bob</NavLink>
```

This page links to the user pages for Alice and Bob using route parameters.

NavMenu.razor **(Update)**

```
<NavLink href="/" class="nav-link" activeClass="active">Home</NavLink>
<NavLink href="/user/Visitor" class="nav-link"
activeClass="active">User</NavLink>
```

These navigation links appear in your app's layout and allow users to jump between home and the user route.

MINI QUIZ: ROUTING AND NAVIGATION

1. What directive associates a Razor component with a URL path?

   o   A) @route

   o   B) @page

   o   C) @url

   o   D) @path

2. What component is used to create a styled navigation link?

   o   A) Link

   o   B) RouterLink

   o   C) NavLink

   o   D) Anchor

3. Which service is used to navigate programmatically in Blazor?

   o   A) RouteService

   o   B) NavigationHelper

   o   C) NavigationManager

   o   D) RouteEngine

Answers:

1. B
2. C
3. C

Objective: Practice creating multiple pages, routing between them, and handling route parameters dynamically.

Steps:

- Add three new Razor components to the *Pages* folder: *Welcome.razor*, *About.razor*, and *Profile.razor*.

- Define routes for each page:

    o */welcome* for *Welcome.razor*

    o */about* for *About.razor*

    o */profile/{name}* for *Profile.razor*

- In *Profile.razor*, display a personalized greeting using the *name* parameter.

- Update *NavMenu.razor* with links to each page using *<NavLink>*.

☑ Bonus Challenge:

In *Profile.razor*, if the *name* parameter is missing or empty, redirect the user to */welcome* using *NavigationManager*.

CHAPTER 7: FORMS AND VALIDATION

Forms are essential to most applications, allowing users to input and submit data. In Blazor, working with forms is streamlined and powerful thanks to built-in components, two-way binding, and robust validation support.

In this chapter, you'll:

- Create and handle forms using Blazor components

- Apply built-in validation with data annotations

- Build custom validation logic

Creating a Blazor Form

Blazor provides several form-related components:

- *EditForm* – the wrapper that manages form submission

- *InputText, InputNumber, InputSelect*, etc. – form controls with binding support

- *ValidationSummary* and *ValidationMessage* – display validation errors

Example:

```
@rendermode InteractiveServer

<EditForm Model="user" OnValidSubmit="HandleValidSubmit"
FormName="basicForm">
    <InputText id="name" @bind-Value="user.Name" />
    <ValidationMessage For="@(() => user.Name)" />
    <button type="submit">Submit</button>
</EditForm>

@code {
    private UserModel user = new();

    void HandleValidSubmit()
    {
        Console.WriteLine($"Submitted: {user.Name}");
    }
```

```
public class UserModel
{
    public string Name { get; set; }
}
}
```

Adding Validation with Data Annotations

To enable validation, decorate your model properties with data annotation attributes.

Example:

```
public class UserModel
{
    [Required(ErrorMessage = "Name is required")]
    [StringLength(50)]
    public string Name { get; set; }

    [EmailAddress]
    public string Email { get; set; }
}
```

Then add the *DataAnnotationsValidator* component inside your form to activate validation support:

```
<EditForm OnSubmit="ValidateManually" FormName="manualForm">
<DataAnnotationsValidator />
    <ValidationSummary />

    <InputText id="name" @bind-Value="user.Name" />
    <ValidationMessage For="@(() => user.Name)" />

    <InputText id="email" @bind-Value="user.Email" />
    <ValidationMessage For="@(() => user.Email)" />

    <button type="submit">Submit</button>
</EditForm>
```

Custom Validation Logic

If you need validation beyond data annotations, you can implement *IValidator* or write manual logic during submission.

Manual Validation Example:

```
<EditForm OnSubmit="ValidateManually">
    <InputText @bind-Value="inputValue" />
    <p>@errorMessage</p>
    <button type="submit">Submit</button>
</EditForm>

@code {
    private string inputValue;
    private string errorMessage;

    void ValidateManually()
    {
        if (string.IsNullOrWhiteSpace(inputValue))
        {
            errorMessage = "Value cannot be empty.";
        }
        else
        {
            errorMessage = string.Empty;
        }
    }
}
```

Now that you understand forms and validation in Blazor, you're equipped to build powerful and user-friendly data-entry workflows. In the next chapter, you'll explore dependency injection and how to organize services cleanly across your app.

FULL EXAMPLE: USER REGISTRATION FORM WITH VALIDATION

This full example demonstrates how to build a user registration form using *EditForm*, built-in input components, and data annotation validation. It combines everything you've learned in this chapter.

Register.razor

```
@page "/register"
@rendermode InteractiveServer
@using System.ComponentModel.DataAnnotations

<h3>User Registration</h3>

<EditForm Model="@registerModel" FormName="registerForm"
OnValidSubmit="HandleValidSubmit">
    <DataAnnotationsValidator />
    <ValidationSummary />

    <div class="form-group mb-3">
        <label for="name">Name</label>
        <InputText id="name" class="form-control" @bind-
Value="registerModel.Name" />
        <ValidationMessage For="@(() => registerModel.Name)" />
    </div>

    <div class="form-group mb-3">
        <label for="email">Email</label>
        <InputText id="email" class="form-control" @bind-
Value="registerModel.Email" />
        <ValidationMessage For="@(() => registerModel.Email)" />
    </div>

    <div class="form-group mb-3">
        <label for="password">Password</label>
        <InputText id="password" class="form-control" type="password" @bind-
Value="registerModel.Password" />
        <ValidationMessage For="@(() => registerModel.Password)" />
    </div>

    <button type="submit" class="btn btn-success">Register</button>
</EditForm>

@if (isSubmitted)
{
    <div class="alert alert-success mt-3">
        Welcome, @registerModel.Name! Your account has been created.
    </div>
```

```csharp
}

@code {
    private RegisterModel registerModel = new();
    private bool isSubmitted = false;

    private void HandleValidSubmit()
    {
        isSubmitted = true;
        Console.WriteLine($"Registered: {registerModel.Name},
{registerModel.Email}");
    }

    public class RegisterModel
    {
        [Required(ErrorMessage = "Name is required")]
        public string Name { get; set; }

        [Required(ErrorMessage = "Email is required"),
EmailAddress(ErrorMessage = "Invalid email format")]
        public string Email { get; set; }

        [Required(ErrorMessage = "Password is required"), StringLength(100,
MinimumLength = 6, ErrorMessage = "Password must be at least 6 characters")]
        public string Password { get; set; }
    }
}
```

MINI QUIZ: FORMS AND VALIDATION

1. What component is required to trigger Blazor's built-in validation?

    o   A) ValidationTrigger

    o   B) DataAnnotationsValidator

    o   C) FormController

    o   D) Validator

2. How do you show a single field's validation message?

    o   A) ValidationSummary

    o   B) ValidationText

    o   C) ValidationMessage

    o   D) ErrorLabel

3. What event should be used for handling valid form submission?

    o   A) OnSubmit

    o   B) OnChange

    o   C) OnValidSubmit

    o   D) OnClick

Answers:

4. B
5. C
6. C

ACTIVITY: BUILD A NEWSLETTER SIGNUP FORM

Objective: Create a newsletter signup form with validation and confirmation messaging.

Steps:

- Create a new component named *NewsletterSignup.razor*.

- Add fields for **Name** and **Email**.

- Use *EditForm*, *InputText*, *DataAnnotationsValidator*, and *ValidationMessage* for validation.

- Display a thank-you message upon successful submission.

☑ Bonus Challenge:

Add a checkbox labeled *"I agree to the terms"* and make it required before allowing form submission.

Dependency Injection (DI) is a key technique for creating modular, maintainable, and testable applications. Blazor uses the built-in DI container from ASP.NET to manage services and their lifetimes.

In this chapter, you'll:

- Understand Dependency Injection concepts

- Register and configure services in Blazor

- Inject services into components

- Explore service lifetimes (Scoped, Singleton, Transient)

What is Dependency Injection?

Dependency Injection is a design pattern that allows components to receive services from a central container rather than creating them manually. This leads to more modular code and simplifies testing and reuse.

In Blazor, the DI container is built into the framework and configured in *Program.cs*.

Registering Services

Services must be registered before you can use them. This is typically done in *Program.cs* after creating the builder and before calling *builder.Build()*.

```
builder.Services.AddScoped<UserService>();
builder.Services.AddSingleton<AppState>();
builder.Services.AddTransient<LoggingService>();
```

You can register services with three lifetimes:

- **Singleton** – A single instance is used across the app's lifetime.

- **Scoped** – One instance per user session (ideal for Blazor Server).

- **Transient** – A new instance is created every time the service is requested.

Injecting Services into Components

Once registered, services can be injected into components using the *@inject* directive:

```
@inject UserService User

<h3>Hello, @User.CurrentUserName</h3>
```

Alternatively, inject them in the *@code* block using the *[Inject]* attribute:

```
@code {
    [Inject] private LoggingService Logger { get; set; }

    protected override void OnInitialized()
    {
        Logger.Log("Component initialized");
    }
}
```

Scoped, Singleton, and Transient Services Explained

Understanding when to use each service lifetime is important for performance and correctness:

- **Singleton**: Shared across the entire application. Good for global data or configuration settings.

- **Scoped**: Unique to each user session. Ideal for user-specific state or services in Blazor Server apps.

- **Transient**: A new instance each time it's injected. Best for lightweight, stateless operations.

You're now equipped to use Dependency Injection effectively in your Blazor applications. In the next chapter, you'll learn how to call REST APIs and fetch dynamic data to power your app.

FULL EXAMPLE: INJECTING AND USING A WEATHER FORECAST SERVICE

This example shows how to build a simple service, register it for dependency injection, and use it in a component. You'll create a weather service that returns a random forecast and display the result in a Blazor component.

WeatherService.cs

```
public class WeatherService
{
    private static readonly string[] Forecasts = new[]
    {
        "Sunny", "Cloudy", "Rainy", "Windy", "Stormy"
    };

    private readonly Random random = new();

    public string GetForecast()
    {
        return Forecasts[random.Next(Forecasts.Length)];
    }
}
```

Register the Service in *Program.cs*

```
builder.Services.AddScoped<WeatherService>();
```

Weather.razor

```
@page "/weather"
@rendermode InteractiveServer
@inject WeatherService WeatherService

<h3>Today's Weather</h3>

<p>The forecast is: <strong>@forecast</strong></p>

<button class="btn btn-primary" @onclick="GetNewForecast">Get New
Forecast</button>
```

```
@code {
    private string forecast;

    protected override void OnInitialized()
    {
        forecast = WeatherService.GetForecast();
    }

    private void GetNewForecast()
    {
        forecast = WeatherService.GetForecast();
    }
}
```

MINI QUIZ: DEPENDENCY INJECTION

1. Which service lifetime creates a single instance throughout the application's lifetime?

   - A) Scoped
   - B) Singleton
   - C) Transient
   - D) Permanent

2. How do you inject a service into a Blazor component using Razor syntax?

   - A) <ServiceInjector>
   - B) @using
   - C) @inject
   - D) @service

3. What is the default service lifetime for Blazor Server?

   - A) Singleton
   - B) Transient
   - C) Scoped
   - D) Session

Answers:

1. B
2. C
3. C

ACTIVITY: CREATE AND INJECT A GREETING SERVICE

Objective: Practice building a reusable service and using dependency injection to display a personalized greeting in a Blazor component.

Steps:

    Step 1: Create the Service: Create a new class called *GreetingService.cs*. Define a method named *GetGreeting* that accepts a *name* and an optional *prefix* parameter:

```
public class GreetingService
{
    public string GetGreeting(string name, string prefix = "Hello")
    {
        return $"{prefix}, {name}!";
    }
}
```

    Step 2: Register the Service: In *Program.cs*, register your new service using dependency injection as a scoped service.

```
builder.Services.AddScoped<GreetingService>();
```

    Step 3: Create the Component: Add a new component called *Greeting.razor* and inject your *GreetingService*.

    Step 4: Add Input and Button: Provide a text box for entering a name and a button to display the greeting.

    Step 5: Display the Greeting: Use your component logic to display the greeting returned by your service on the page when the button is clicked.

☑ Bonus Challenge:

Enhance the component with a dropdown list of greeting styles *("Hello", "Hi", "Welcome",* etc.), and allow the user to select one before submitting. Pass the selected style to the service for a customized message.

Modern web applications often need to interact with external APIs to fetch or manipulate data. Blazor makes this process seamless by providing built-in support for HTTP-based communication.

In this chapter, you'll learn how to:

- Configure an HTTP client in Blazor
- Fetch data from REST APIs
- Perform CRUD operations
- Handle API errors gracefully

HTTP Client Configuration

Blazor uses *HttpClient* to communicate with external APIs.

- **In Blazor WebAssembly**, *HttpClient* is preconfigured using the browser's Fetch API.

- **In Blazor Server**, you must register it manually in *Program.cs*:

```
builder.Services.AddHttpClient();
```

Then inject it into your component using:

```
@inject HttpClient Http
```

Fetching Data from REST APIs

Here's how to fetch data from an API endpoint:

```
@inject HttpClient Http

@if (users == null)
{
    <p>Loading...</p>
}
else
{
    <ul>
        @foreach (var user in users)
        {
            <li>@user.Name (@user.Email)</li>
        }
    </ul>
}

@code {
    private User[] users;

    protected override async Task OnInitializedAsync()
    {
        users = await
Http.GetFromJsonAsync<User[]>("https://example.com/api/users");
    }

    public class User
    {
        public string Name { get; set; }
        public string Email { get; set; }
    }
}
```

Performing CRUD Operations

Blazor supports all standard REST verbs:

- **Create** – *PostAsJsonAsync(url, data)*

- **Read** – *GetFromJsonAsync<T>(url)*

- **Update** – *PutAsJsonAsync(url, data)*

- **Delete** – *DeleteAsync(url)*

Example: Creating a New User

Here's how you can create a new user by posting data to an API:

```
<button @onclick="CreateUser">Add User</button>

@code {
    async Task CreateUser()
    {
        var newUser = new User { Name = "Jane Doe", Email =
"jane@example.com" };
        await Http.PostAsJsonAsync("https://example.com/api/users",
newUser);
    }
}
```

Handling API Errors and Responses

Always handle potential errors during API communication to avoid unhandled exceptions and poor user experiences.

Example: Basic Error Handling

```
@code {
    private User[] users;
    private string errorMessage;

    protected override async Task OnInitializedAsync()
    {
        try
        {
            var response = await
Http.GetAsync("https://example.com/api/users");
            if (response.IsSuccessStatusCode)
            {
                users = await response.Content.ReadFromJsonAsync<User[]>();
            }
            else
            {
                errorMessage = "Unable to load users.";
            }
        }
        catch (Exception ex)
        {
            errorMessage = $"Error: {ex.Message}";
```

```
            }
        }
}

@if (!string.IsNullOrEmpty(errorMessage))
{
    <p class="text-danger">@errorMessage</p>
}
```

FULL EXAMPLE: FETCH AND DISPLAY USER DATA FROM AN API

This example shows how to use *HttpClient* to retrieve and display data from a REST API in a Blazor component. You'll build a simple user list that loads from a public test API.

Register *HttpClient in Program.cs* (Blazor Server Only)

If you're using Blazor Server, ensure *HttpClient* is registered:

```
builder.Services.AddHttpClient();
```

For **Blazor WebAssembly**, *HttpClient* is already preconfigured.

UserList.razor

```
@page "/users"
@inject HttpClient Http

<h3>User List</h3>

@if (users == null)
{
    <p>Loading users...</p>
}
else if (users.Length == 0)
{
    <p>No users found.</p>
}
else
{
    <ul>
        @foreach (var user in users)
        {
            <li><strong>@user.Name</strong> - @user.Email</li>
        }
    </ul>
}

@code {
    private User[] users;

    protected override async Task OnInitializedAsync()
    {
        try
        {
```

```
            users = await Http.GetFromJsonAsync<User[]>(
                "https://jsonplaceholder.typicode.com/users");
        }
        catch (Exception ex)
        {
            Console.WriteLine($"Error fetching users: {ex.Message}");
        }
    }

    public class User
    {
        public string Name { get; set; }
        public string Email { get; set; }
    }
}
```

1. **Which method is used to retrieve data from an API as JSON?**

   - o   A) GetData()

   - o   B) GetJsonAsync()

   - o   C) GetFromJsonAsync()

   - o   D) ReadJson()

2. **What HTTP method should you use to create a new resource via an API?**

   - o   A) GET

   - o   B) POST

   - o   C) PUT

   - o   D) DELETE

3. **To handle errors during API calls, you should use:**

   - o   A) An event handler

   - o   B) Try-catch blocks

   - o   C) Exception annotations

   - o   D) Error components

Answers:

1. C
2. B
3. B

Objective: Practice using *HttpClient* to retrieve and display content from an external REST API.

Steps:

- Create a new Razor component named *PostViewer.razor*

- Use *HttpClient* to fetch data from: *https://jsonplaceholder.typicode.com/posts*

- Display the **title** and **body** of each post in a styled card or list

- Show a **loading** message while the data is being retrieved

☑ Bonus Challenge:

- Add a "**Refresh Posts**" button that re-fetches the posts when clicked

- Optionally, **limit the list** to the first five posts or allow the user to select how many to view

Security is vital for any web application. Blazor provides built-in support for **authentication** (verifying user identity) and **authorization** (controlling access based on roles or policies).

In this chapter, you will:

- Understand authentication and authorization concepts
- Implement authentication in Blazor
- Use role-based authorization
- Protect components and routes

Understanding Authentication and Authorization

- **Authentication** identifies who the user is (login process).

- **Authorization** determines what resources a user can access (permissions and roles).

Setting Up Authentication

Blazor supports multiple authentication providers, including:

- **ASP.NET Core Identity** (for individual user accounts)

- **Azure Active Directory (Azure AD)**

- **Third-party OAuth providers** (e.g., Google, Facebook, GitHub)

Example (ASP.NET Core Identity setup in *Program.cs*):

```
builder.Services.AddAuthentication().AddCookie();
builder.Services.AddAuthorization();
```

For Blazor Server, authentication is typically configured using cookies. For Blazor WebAssembly, authentication is often handled via tokens.

Using Authentication State Provider

To check the current user's authentication state within a component:

```
@inject AuthenticationStateProvider AuthStateProvider

@code {
    protected override async Task OnInitializedAsync()
    {
        var authState = await
AuthStateProvider.GetAuthenticationStateAsync();
        var user = authState.User;

        if (user.Identity?.IsAuthenticated == true)
        {
            // User is logged in
        }
    }
}
```

Role-Based Authorization

Roles allow you to restrict access based on user categories (e.g., Admin, Manager, User).

Secure an entire component:

```
@attribute [Authorize(Roles = "Admin")]

<h3>Admin Panel</h3>
```

Or check role in code:

```
if (user.IsInRole("Admin"))
{
    // Allow access
}
```

Protecting Components and Routes

To restrict access to authenticated users:

```
@page "/secure"
@attribute [Authorize]

<h3>Secure Page</h3>
<p>Only authenticated users can access this page.</p>
```

You can also use *[Authorize(Roles = "Manager")]* to limit access further.

FULL EXAMPLE: SIMULATED LOGIN WITH CONDITIONAL ACCESS

This example demonstrates a basic approach to simulating authentication in a Blazor app. You'll use a simple fake login model, conditionally show content based on user status, and simulate roles without connecting to an identity provider.

FakeAuthService.cs

```
public class FakeAuthService
{
    public string CurrentUser { get; private set; }
    public bool IsLoggedIn => !string.IsNullOrEmpty(CurrentUser);

    public void Login(string username)
    {
        CurrentUser = username;
    }

    public void Logout()
    {
        CurrentUser = null;
    }
}
```

Register the Service in *Program.cs*

```
builder.Services.AddScoped<FakeAuthService>();
```

Login.razor

```
@page "/login"
@inject FakeAuthService AuthService
@inject NavigationManager Nav

<h3>Login</h3>

@if (!AuthService.IsLoggedIn)
{
    <input @bind="username" placeholder="Enter your username" class="form-control" />
```

```
        <button class="btn btn-success mt-2"
@onclick="HandleLogin">Login</button>
}
else
{
    <p>You are already logged in as
<strong>@AuthService.CurrentUser</strong>.</p>
    <button class="btn btn-danger" @onclick="HandleLogout">Logout</button>
}

@code {
    private string username;

    private void HandleLogin()
    {
        AuthService.Login(username);
        Nav.NavigateTo("/secure");
    }

    private void HandleLogout()
    {
        AuthService.Logout();
        Nav.NavigateTo("/");
    }
}
```

SecurePage.razor

```
@page "/secure"
@inject FakeAuthService AuthService

<h3>Secure Content</h3>

@if (!AuthService.IsLoggedIn)
{
    <p>Please <a href="/login">log in</a> to view this content.</p>
}
else
{
    <p>Welcome, <strong>@AuthService.CurrentUser</strong>! You now have
access to this protected area.</p>
}
```

MINI QUIZ: AUTHENTICATION AND AUTHORIZATION

1. **What process identifies a user's identity?**

   - o A) Authentication
   - o B) Authorization
   - o C) Validation
   - o D) Verification

2. **What attribute secures Blazor components?**

   - o A) [Protected]
   - o B) [Authorize]
   - o C) [Secure]
   - o D) [Authenticated]

3. **Which provider helps determine the current user's authentication state?**

   - o A) UserProvider
   - o B) AuthorizationProvider
   - o C) IdentityProvider
   - o D) AuthenticationStateProvider

Answers:

1. A
2. B
3. D

ACTIVITY: SIMULATE A ROLE-BASED GREETING

Objective: Practice simulating a basic login process and displaying role-specific content in a Blazor component.

Steps:

- Create a service named *RoleAuthService* with two properties: *Username* and *Role*

- Add a method *Login(string username, string role)* that sets both properties

- Create a page called *RoleLogin.razor* with two input fields: one for the username and one for the role

- Display different greetings based on the entered role *("admin"*, *"staff"*, or *"guest"*)

☑ Bonus Challenge:

If the user enters an unsupported role, display a warning message and prevent login until a valid role is provided.

Blazor allows seamless interaction with JavaScript libraries through JavaScript Interoperability (JS Interop). JS Interop is useful for integrating existing JavaScript functionality or accessing browser APIs directly from your Blazor application.

In this chapter, you'll learn how to:

- Understand the purpose of JS Interop

- Invoke JavaScript functions from Blazor

- Call Blazor methods from JavaScript

Understanding JavaScript Interoperability

JS Interop bridges Blazor's .NET runtime and JavaScript, enabling developers to reuse existing JavaScript libraries and interact directly with browser APIs not yet available via native .NET.

Invoking JavaScript from Blazor

Creating a JavaScript File

First, create a JavaScript file within your project's *wwwroot* folder.

In Visual Studio:

- Right-click *wwwroot*

- Choose **Add → New Item**

- Select **JavaScript File**

- Name it *site.js*

This file holds custom JavaScript functions your Blazor app will call.

Step 1: Add a JavaScript Function (*wwwroot/site.js*):

```
function showAlert(message) {
    alert(message);
}
```

Step 2: Reference the Script in Your Layout

In your *MainLayout.razor*, include the script just after the *@inherits LayoutComponentBase* line:

```
<HeadContent>
    <script src="site.js"></script>
</HeadContent>
```

Step 3: Call JavaScript from Blazor

Inside your Razor component:

```
@inject IJSRuntime JS
@rendermode InteractiveServer

<button @onclick="ShowAlert">Show Alert</button>

@code {
    async Task ShowAlert()
    {
        await JS.InvokeVoidAsync("showAlert", "Hello from Blazor!");
    }
}
```

Calling Blazor from JavaScript

Blazor supports calling .NET methods directly from JavaScript by marking them with *[JSInvokable]*. Such methods must be static because JavaScript needs to access them at the class level without an instance.

Step 1: Define a Blazor Component Method

Define a static method within your Blazor component to be callable from JavaScript:

```
<h3>@message</h3>

@code {
    private static Action<string> NotifyMessageChanged;
    private string message;

    protected override void OnInitialized()
    {
        NotifyMessageChanged = (msg) =>
        {
            message = msg;
            StateHasChanged();
        };
    }

    [JSInvokable]
    public static void UpdateMessage(string newMessage)
    {
        NotifyMessageChanged?.Invoke(newMessage);
    }
}
```

Step 2: Invoke from JavaScript

In your *site.js* file (or any JavaScript context), call the Blazor method:

```
DotNet.invokeMethodAsync('YourBlazorAssembly', 'UpdateMessage', 'Hello from JavaScript!');
```

Replace *'YourBlazorAssembly'* with the exact assembly name of your Blazor project (typically your project's name).

Additional Tips

- **Handling JavaScript Promises:**
  Blazor allows you to interact with JavaScript functions that return promises. Here's an example of retrieving a value asynchronously from JavaScript:

```
var userName = await JS.InvokeAsync<string>("prompt", "Enter your name:");
```

- **Debugging JS Interop Issues:**
  If you're encountering issues with JS Interop calls, always check your browser's developer console (*F12* or *Ctrl+Shift+J*) for detailed error messages and logs.

FULL EXAMPLE: SCROLL TO TOP WITH JAVASCRIPT

This example demonstrates how to call a JavaScript function from a Blazor component using *IJSRuntime*, tailored to the .NET 9 Blazor Web App structure.

1. Create the JavaScript File: *wwwroot/site.js*

```
window.scrollToTop = () => window.scrollTo({ top: 0, behavior: 'smooth' });
```

2. Reference the Script in *MainLayout.razor*

```
<HeadContent>
    <script src="site.js"></script>
</HeadContent>
```

3. Razor Component: *ScrollDemo.razor*

```
@page "/scroll"
@inject IJSRuntime JS

<button class="btn btn-primary" @onclick="ScrollToTop">Scroll to
Top</button>

@code {
    async Task ScrollToTop() =>
        await JS.InvokeVoidAsync("scrollToTop");
}
```

MINI QUIZ: JAVASCRIPT INTEROPERABILITY

1. **What service is used to call JavaScript methods from Blazor?**

   - A) JavaScriptInvoker

   - B) JSInterop

   - C) IJSRuntime

   - D) JSService

2. **Which attribute makes Blazor methods callable from JavaScript?**

   - A) [JSCallable]

   - B) [JSInterop]

   - C) [JSMethod]

   - D) [JSInvokable]

3. **How do you invoke a JavaScript method asynchronously from Blazor?**

   - A) InvokeVoid

   - B) InvokeAsync

   - C) InvokeSync

   - D) CallJavaScript

Answers:

1. C
2. D
3. B

ACTIVITY: DISPLAY THE CURRENT TIME USING JAVASCRIPT

Objective: Use JavaScript interop to fetch and display the current time from JavaScript instead of C#.

Steps:

1. **Add a JavaScript function** to *wwwroot/site.js*:

```
window.getCurrentTime = () => {
    return new Date().toLocaleTimeString();
};
```

2. **Create a component** named *TimeDisplay.razor*.

3. Inject *IJSRuntime* and call *getCurrentTime* when the user clicks a "**Get Time**" button.

4. Display the time on the page using a local C# variable.

☑ **Bonus Challenge:**

Add a timer that refreshes the time every 10 seconds using *Timer* and *JS.InvokeAsync*.

Now that you're comfortable with basic Blazor components, it's time to explore advanced techniques that unlock greater **flexibility**, **reusability**, and **control**.

In this chapter, you'll learn how to:

- Understand and utilize *RenderFragment* and template components.

- Reference and manipulate component instances using *@ref*.

- Handle complex event scenarios using *EventCallback*.

- Implement comprehensive error handling within components.

RenderFragment and Template Components

In Blazor, a *RenderFragment* is a piece of UI content defined as a reusable template. It enables powerful component designs with customizable layouts.

Example: Creating Template Components

Define a templated component called *AlertComponent.razor*:

```
<div class="alert alert-@AlertType">
    @ChildContent
</div>

@code {
    [Parameter] public RenderFragment ChildContent { get; set; }
    [Parameter] public string AlertType { get; set; } = "info";
}
```

Usage:

```
<AlertComponent AlertType="success">
    <strong>Success!</strong> Your operation completed successfully.
</AlertComponent>

<AlertComponent AlertType="warning">
    <strong>Warning!</strong> Check your inputs.
</AlertComponent>
```

Using *@ref* to Reference Components

Blazor provides the *@ref* directive to create references to component instances, enabling you to invoke their methods or access properties directly.

Example: Using *@ref*

Create a child component *CounterComponent.razor*:

```
<h4>Current count: @count</h4>

@code {
    private int count;

    public void IncrementCount() => count++;
}
```

Use *@ref* in the parent component:

```
<CounterComponent @ref="counterRef" />

<button @onclick="IncrementChildCounter">Increment Child Counter</button>

@code {
    private CounterComponent counterRef;

    private void IncrementChildCounter()
    {
        counterRef.IncrementCount();
    }
}
```

Handling Events with *EventCallback*

EventCallback is Blazor's strongly-typed delegate mechanism for component events, making components reusable and maintaining clear separation of concerns.

Example: Child-to-Parent Communication

Child component (*ChildComponent.razor*):

```
<button @onclick="NotifyParent">Notify Parent</button>

@code {
    [Parameter] public EventCallback<string> OnNotify { get; set; }

    private async Task NotifyParent()
    {
        await OnNotify.InvokeAsync("Message from Child!");
    }
}
```

Parent component usage:

```
<ChildComponent OnNotify="HandleNotification" />

<p>@notificationMessage</p>

@code {
    private string notificationMessage;

    private void HandleNotification(string message)
    {
        notificationMessage = message;
    }
}
```

Error Handling in Components

Robust applications must gracefully handle errors. Blazor provides lifecycle methods and mechanisms to handle exceptions effectively.

Using *ErrorBoundary*

The *ErrorBoundary* component, introduced in .NET 6, catches and handles errors gracefully within your component hierarchy.

Example:

```
<ErrorBoundary>
    <ChildContent>
        <ProblematicComponent />
    </ChildContent>
    <ErrorContent>
        <p>Something went wrong. Please refresh or contact support.</p>
    </ErrorContent>
</ErrorBoundary>
```

Overriding *OnErrorAsync*

Custom error-handling can be achieved by overriding the component's lifecycle method *OnErrorAsync*.

```
@code {
    protected override Task OnErrorAsync(Exception exception)
    {
        Console.WriteLine($"Error encountered: {exception.Message}");
        return base.OnErrorAsync(exception);
    }
}
```

FULL EXAMPLE: REUSABLE MODAL DIALOG WITH RENDERFRAGMENT AND EVENTCALLBACK

This example demonstrates how to build a **reusable modal dialog** in Blazor using *RenderFragment* to pass content and EventCallback to communicate events back to the parent. It's a powerful pattern for modular UI design.

Modal.razor **(Reusable Component)**

```
<div class="modal-background" @onclick="Close">
    <div class="modal-content" @onclick:stopPropagation>
        @ChildContent
        <button class="btn btn-sm btn-danger mt-2"
@onclick="Close">Close</button>
    </div>
</div>

@code {
    [Parameter] public RenderFragment ChildContent { get; set; }
    [Parameter] public EventCallback OnClose { get; set; }

    private async Task Close()
    {
        await OnClose.InvokeAsync();
    }
}
```

Add CSS *(Place this in wwwroot/app.css or your main CSS file)*

```
.modal-background {
    position: fixed;
    top: 0; left: 0; right: 0; bottom: 0;
    background-color: rgba(0, 0, 0, 0.6);
    display: flex;
    justify-content: center;
    align-items: center;
}

.modal-content {
    background: white;
    padding: 20px;
    border-radius: 8px;
    min-width: 300px;
}
```

ModalDemo.razor

```
@page "/modal"
@rendermode InteractiveServer

<h3>Modal Demo</h3>

<button class="btn btn-primary" @onclick="ShowModal">Open Modal</button>

@if (isOpen)
{
    <Modal OnClose="HideModal">
        <h4>This is modal content!</h4>
        <p>You can place any custom markup here.</p>
    </Modal>
}

@code {
    private bool isOpen = false;

    void ShowModal() => isOpen = true;
    void HideModal() => isOpen = false;
}
```

This pattern is excellent for dialogs, confirmation prompts, or any content that needs to be displayed over the current UI. You've now built a flexible component that can be reused across your entire app.

MINI QUIZ: ADVANCED COMPONENT CONCEPTS

1. **What directive allows you to access component instances directly?**

   - A) @bind
   - B) @ref
   - C) @bind-instance
   - D) @instance

2. **Which delegate type enables strongly-typed event handling in Blazor components?**

   - A) DelegateCallback
   - B) EventHandler
   - C) EventCallback
   - D) CallbackEvent

3. **Which Blazor feature helps manage errors gracefully in components?**

   - A) @try
   - B) ErrorBoundary
   - C) ErrorHandler
   - D) ExceptionBoundary

Answers:

1. B
2. C
3. B

ACTIVITY: BUILD A REUSABLE NOTIFICATION BANNER

Objective: Use advanced component patterns to create a flexible notification banner that displays dynamic content and can be dismissed by the user.

Steps:

- Create a new component named *Notification.razor*.

- Accept a *RenderFragment* to allow dynamic message content.

- Add a **Dismiss** button that triggers an *EventCallback* to notify the parent when it's closed.

- On a demo page, use the component to show both a success and an error message.

☑ Bonus Challenge:

Add a *BackgroundColor* parameter so the parent component can control the banner's background color (e.g., green for success, red for error).

Blazor applications become truly engaging when you leverage effective styling techniques.

In this chapter, you'll enhance the visual appeal and usability of your apps:

- Apply styles effectively to your Blazor components.

- Isolate component-specific styles using CSS isolation.

- Incorporate popular CSS frameworks like Bootstrap into your project.

- Build responsive user interfaces optimized for multiple devices.

Adding Global Styles in Blazor

Blazor uses standard CSS for styling. You can define **global styles** that apply across the entire application.

Example:

Create a new file: *wwwroot/css/site.css*

```
body {
    font-family: 'Segoe UI', Arial, sans-serif;
    background-color: #f8f9fa;
}

button {
    border-radius: 5px;
}
```

Include your stylesheet by editing your *wwwroot/index.html* file:

```
<link href="css/site.css" rel="stylesheet" />
```

CSS Isolation

CSS Isolation in Blazor helps you avoid style conflicts by encapsulating styles specifically within components.

How it works:

1. Create a CSS file named after the component, with *.razor.css* suffix.
   For *ButtonComponent.razor*, create *ButtonComponent.razor.css*:

```css
.primary-button {
    background-color: blue;
    color: white;
    padding: 10px;
}
```

2. Apply your isolated style directly within your component:

```html
<button class="primary-button">Click Me</button>
```

These styles only affect *ButtonComponent*, not other components.

Integrating Bootstrap into Blazor

Bootstrap is a popular framework that helps you quickly build clean, responsive UIs.

Step 1: Include Bootstrap

Add this line to your *index.html*:

```html
<link
href="https://cdn.jsdelivr.net/npm/bootstrap@5.3.2/dist/css/bootstrap.min.cs
s" rel="stylesheet" />
```

Step 2: Using Bootstrap Classes:

```
<div class="container">
    <button class="btn btn-primary">Bootstrap Button</button>
</div>
```

Responsive Design Essentials

Creating a responsive design ensures your app provides a great user experience on various screen sizes.

- Utilize Bootstrap's responsive grid classes (*col-md*, *col-lg*, etc.).

- Leverage CSS Flexbox and Grid layouts for advanced responsiveness.

- Employ CSS media queries to adjust styles based on screen size:

```
@media (max-width: 768px) {
    .sidebar {
        display: none;
    }
}
```

FULL EXAMPLE: THEMED DASHBOARD PANEL WITH RESPONSIVE CSS

This example demonstrates how to build a visually styled dashboard panel using CSS isolation. The layout adapts to different screen sizes, showcasing responsive design best practices.

Step 1: Create *DashboardPanel.razor*

```
<div class="dashboard-panel">
    <h2>@Title</h2>
    <p>@Description</p>
</div>

@code {
    [Parameter] public string Title { get; set; }
    [Parameter] public string Description { get; set; }
}
```

Step 2: Create *DashboardPanel.razor.css*

```
.dashboard-panel {
    padding: 1.5rem;
    border: 1px solid #e0e0e0;
    background-color: #ffffff;
    border-radius: 8px;
    box-shadow: 0 2px 5px rgba(0,0,0,0.1);
    margin-bottom: 1rem;
}

.dashboard-panel h2 {
    margin-top: 0;
    color: #007acc;
}

@media (max-width: 600px) {
    .dashboard-panel {
        padding: 1rem;
        font-size: 0.9rem;
    }
}
```

MINI QUIZ: STYLING AND RESPONSIVE DESIGN

1. **To isolate CSS styles for a component named *MyCard.razor*, what filename should you use?**

   o   A) MyCard.css

   o   B) MyCard.styles.css

   o   C) MyCard.razor.css

   o   D) MyCard.component.css

2. **How do you reference global CSS files in a Blazor application?**

   o   A) Using JavaScript Interop

   o   B) Inside _Imports.razor

   o   C) Within index.html

   o   D) Directly in components only

3. **Which framework provides built-in classes for responsive layout?**

   o   A) Tailwind or Bootstrap

   o   B) jQuery

   o   C) AngularJS

   o   D) Razor Components

Answers:

   1. C
   2. C
   3. A

ACTIVITY: BUILD A STYLED, RESPONSIVE PROFILE CARD

Objective: Create a reusable profile card component with responsive design using CSS isolation and a CSS framework like Bootstrap.

Steps:

1. Create a new component named *ProfileCard.razor*.

2. Add *[Parameter]* properties for *Name*, *Title*, and *ImageUrl*.

3. Design the layout using Bootstrap classes or CSS Flexbox for clean alignment.

4. Create a *ProfileCard.razor.css* file and apply custom styles (e.g., border, padding, hover effects).

5. Add a media query to adjust the layout or font size for screens smaller than 600px.

6. Display the profile card on your homepage or in a test component for preview.

☑ Bonus Challenge:

Add a *BackgroundColor* parameter and implement support for light and dark themes with a toggle button.

CHAPTER 14: PERFORMANCE OPTIMIZATION

As your Blazor applications grow more complex and powerful, maintaining optimal performance becomes essential for user satisfaction.

In this chapter, you'll learn to:

- Measure and understand your application's performance.

- Implement lazy loading for improved startup speed.

- Optimize rendering and minimize unnecessary UI updates.

- Use data virtualization techniques to efficiently handle large datasets.

Measuring Performance in Blazor Applications

Before optimizing, it's essential to measure and identify bottlenecks. Browser developer tools provide valuable insights into performance:

- **Browser DevTools** (e.g., Chrome DevTools):

  - Use the **Performance** tab to record and analyze load times and rendering performance.

  - Identify slow operations and unnecessary rendering cycles.

- **.NET profiling tools** (e.g., Visual Studio Diagnostics):

  - Monitor application startup, memory usage, and CPU utilization.

Quick Reference Essentials:

- Regularly profile your Blazor apps during development.

- Identify and prioritize performance bottlenecks before optimization.

Lazy Loading Components and Assemblies

Lazy loading defers loading components and assemblies until necessary, significantly reducing initial load times.

How to Implement Lazy Loading:

1. **Mark assemblies for lazy loading** in your Blazor WebAssembly project file (*.csproj*):

```
<ItemGroup>
  <BlazorWebAssemblyLazyLoad Include="YourLargeAssembly.dll" />
</ItemGroup>
```

2. **Trigger loading** in your component:

```
@page "/lazy"
@inject LazyAssemblyLoader loader

<button @onclick="LoadComponent">Load Heavy Component</button>

@if (isLoaded)
{
    <HeavyComponent />
}

@code {
    bool isLoaded = false;

    async Task LoadComponent()
    {
        await loader.LoadAssembliesAsync(new[] { "YourLargeAssembly.dll" });
        isLoaded = true;
    }
}
```

This ensures your application loads quickly by only loading essential resources initially.

Optimizing Rendering Performance

Blazor automatically manages UI rendering but can sometimes re-render excessively, affecting performance.

Use *ShouldRender* to Control Rendering:

Override *ShouldRender* to avoid unnecessary renders:

```
@code {
    private int counter;

    protected override bool ShouldRender()
    {
        // Render only if counter is divisible by 5
        return counter % 5 == 0;
    }

    private void IncrementCounter()
    {
        counter++;
    }
}
```

Quick Reference Essentials:

- Minimize component re-renders by overriding *ShouldRender*.

- Use precise conditional checks to render only when truly necessary.

Data Virtualization

Virtualization efficiently manages large datasets by rendering only the items visible to the user, significantly improving performance and responsiveness.

Implementing Virtualization:

Blazor provides a built-in component for data virtualization:

```
<Virtualize Items="@largeDataset" Context="item">
    <div>@item.Name</div>
</Virtualize>

@code {
    private List<Item> largeDataset;

    protected override async Task OnInitializedAsync()
    {
        // Simulate large dataset
        largeDataset = Enumerable.Range(1, 10000).Select(i => new Item {
Name = $"Item {i}" }).ToList();
    }

    class Item
    {
        public string Name { get; set; }
    }
}
```

This significantly improves load and scroll performance for large collections.

You now have powerful strategies at your disposal to keep your Blazor apps performing exceptionally well!

FULL EXAMPLE: VIRTUALIZED PRODUCT LIST WITH OPTIMIZED RENDERING

This example demonstrates how to improve performance when rendering large datasets by combining the *<Virtualize>* component with controlled rendering using *ShouldRender*. You'll generate a large list of sample products and display them using virtualization, minimizing the performance cost of rendering thousands of items.

Step 1: Generate Sample Data

Create a *Product* class and initialize a large list of product entries.

```
@code {
    private List<Product> products;

    protected override void OnInitialized()
    {
        products = Enumerable.Range(1, 5000).Select(i => new Product
        {
            Id = i,
            Name = $"Product {i}",
            Description = $"Description for product {i}"
        }).ToList();
    }

    class Product
    {
        public int Id { get; set; }
        public string Name { get; set; }
        public string Description { get; set; }
    }
}
```

Step 2: Use the *<Virtualize>* Component

Wrap the list in a *<Virtualize>* element to ensure only the visible items are rendered on-screen.

```
<Virtualize Items="@products" Context="product">
    <div class="product-item">
        <h5>@product.Name</h5>
        <p>@product.Description</p>
    </div>
</Virtualize>
```

Step 3: Control Rendering with *ShouldRender*

Override the *ShouldRender* method in the component to control unnecessary re-renders.

```
@code {
    private bool shouldUpdate = false;

    protected override bool ShouldRender() => shouldUpdate;

    private void UpdateProducts()
    {
        // Custom logic for when to allow rendering
        shouldUpdate = true;
    }
}
```

This combination improves performance significantly by rendering only what's needed and avoiding extra UI updates.

MINI QUIZ: PERFORMANCE OPTIMIZATION

1. **Which method can you override to avoid unnecessary component rendering?**

    o A) OnParametersSet

    o B) OnAfterRender

    o C) ShouldRender

    o D) OnInitialized

2. **Lazy loading primarily improves:**

    o A) Component re-rendering efficiency

    o B) Initial application load times

    o C) Memory consumption

    o D) API communication speed

3. **What Blazor component helps efficiently handle large datasets?**

    o A) LazyLoader

    o B) Virtualize

    o C) RenderFragment

    o D) DataGrid

Answers:

1. C
2. B
3. B

ACTIVITY: OPTIMIZE A PRODUCT LISTING PAGE

Objective: Apply performance optimization techniques by combining virtualization and rendering control in a real-world list scenario.

Steps:

1. Create a new Razor component named *ProductList.razor*.

2. Generate a list of 5,000+ sample products using *Enumerable.Range*.

3. Display the product list using the *<Virtualize>* component.

4. Style each product with basic CSS for padding, borders, and spacing.

5. Override *ShouldRender* to control unnecessary updates.

☑ Bonus Challenge:

- Use browser developer tools or Visual Studio Diagnostics to profile your app before and after adding virtualization.

- Add a "Load More Products" button that simulates lazy-loading more entries into the list.

- Try experimenting with virtualization parameters like *ItemSize* or *OverscanCount* to tune scrolling behavior.

Testing your Blazor applications is critical to building reliable, maintainable software. This chapter introduces **bUnit**, a powerful testing library designed specifically for Blazor component testing.

What You'll Learn:

• How to set up a Blazor component test project
• How to write unit tests for Blazor components using bUnit
• How to mock services and dependencies
• How to test component rendering, interaction, and JavaScript interop

Introduction to Testing in Blazor

Testing is essential to verify that components behave as expected. In Blazor, tests ensure that UI logic, component rendering, and interactions are working correctly.

- **Types of tests:**

    o **Unit Tests**: Validate individual methods or logic.

    o **Integration Tests**: Check interactions between components and services.

    o **UI Tests**: Ensure visual correctness and interactions in the browser.

bUnit is specifically designed to simplify Blazor component testing, enabling robust tests without complex setups.

Setting Up bUnit in Visual Studio

To test your Blazor components with bUnit in Visual Studio, follow these steps:

Step 1: Create a New Test Project

1. In **Visual Studio**, right-click on your Blazor solution.

2. Select **Add > New Project...**

3. Search for **xUnit Test Project** and select it.

4. Name the project something like *MyBlazorApp.Tests*.

5. Click **Create**.

Step 2: Add bUnit to the Test Project

1. In the **Solution Explorer**, right-click on the new test project and choose **Manage NuGet Packages**.

2. Go to the **Browse** tab and search for *bunit*.

3. Select the *bunit* package (by Egil Hansen) and click **Install**.

Step 3: Reference Your Main Blazor Project

1. Right-click the **Dependencies** node in the test project.

2. Select **Add Project Reference**.

3. Check the box for your main Blazor project and click **OK**.

You're now ready to write tests for your Blazor components using bUnit in Visual Studio!

Writing Your First Component Test

Create a basic component test with bUnit:

Example Component (*Greeting.razor*):

```
<h3>Hello, @Name!</h3>

@code {
    [Parameter] public string Name { get; set; }
}
```

Test:

```
using Bunit;
using Xunit;

public class GreetingTest
{
    [Fact]
    public void GreetingDisplaysCorrectName()
    {
        using var ctx = new TestContext();

        var component = ctx.RenderComponent<Greeting>(parameters =>
parameters.Add(p => p.Name, "Adam"));

        component.MarkupMatches("<h3>Hello, Adam!</h3>");
    }
}
```

Testing Component Lifecycle and Rendering

Test initial renders, state changes, and re-rendering:

- **Example:** Verify a button click updates state correctly.

Counter Component:

```
<button @onclick="IncrementCount">@count</button>

@code {
    private int count;

    void IncrementCount() => count++;
}
```

Test:

```
[Fact]
public void ClickingButtonIncrementsCount()
{
    using var ctx = new TestContext();
    var component = ctx.RenderComponent<Counter>();
```

```
    component.Find("button").Click();

    component.Find("button").MarkupMatches("<button>1</button>");
}
```

Mocking Dependencies and Services

Use mock frameworks (e.g., Moq) to handle dependencies:

Service Example:

```
public interface IUserService
{
    string GetUserName();
}
```

Component with Service:

```
@inject IUserService UserService

<p>@UserService.GetUserName()</p>
```

Test:

```
using Moq;

[Fact]
public void UserNameDisplayedCorrectly()
{
    var mockService = new Mock<IUserService>();
    mockService.Setup(s => s.GetUserName()).Returns("Adam");

    using var ctx = new TestContext();
    ctx.Services.AddSingleton<IUserService>(mockService.Object);

    var component = ctx.RenderComponent<UserComponent>();

    component.MarkupMatches("<p>Adam</p>");
}
```

Advanced bUnit Testing Techniques

Explore advanced testing scenarios:

- **EventCallbacks:** Test interactions triggered by user actions.

- **JSInterop:** Verify calls to JavaScript from Blazor.

Example: Testing JSInterop:

```
[Fact]
public void ComponentCallsJavaScriptMethod()
{
    using var ctx = new TestContext();
    var jsMock = ctx.JSInterop.SetupVoid("alert", "Hello from Blazor!");

    var component = ctx.RenderComponent<AlertComponent>();

    component.Find("button").Click();

    jsMock.VerifyInvoke("alert");
}
```

This example walks you through writing a test using the **bUnit** testing framework. You'll test a simple *Greeting.razor* component that displays a personalized message, and verify that it renders the correct output using bUnit assertions.

Step 1: Create the Component

Greeting.razor

```
<h3>Hello, @Name!</h3>

@code {
    [Parameter] public string Name { get; set; }
}
```

Step 2: Write the Test

In your bUnit-enabled test project:

GreetingTest.cs

```
using Bunit;
using Xunit;

public class GreetingTest
{
    [Fact]
    public void GreetingDisplaysCorrectName()
    {
        using var ctx = new TestContext();

        var component = ctx.RenderComponent<Greeting>(
            parameters => parameters.Add(p => p.Name, "Adam")
        );

        component.MarkupMatches("<h3>Hello, Adam!</h3>");
    }
}
```

What This Test Does:

- **Renders** the *Greeting* component with *Name = "Adam"*
- **Asserts** that the output HTML exactly matches the expected markup
- **Demonstrates** the simplicity and power of bUnit's fluent testing API

This foundational test pattern can be applied to many other components as you build your suite.

MINI QUIZ: TESTING BLAZOR COMPONENTS

1. **What framework is specifically designed to test Blazor components?**

   - a) NUnit

   - b) xUnit

   - c) bUnit

   - d) MSTest

2. **What bUnit method checks the rendered HTML output of a component?**

   - a) CheckRender

   - b) RenderCheck

   - c) MarkupMatches

   - d) HTMLAssert

3. **Which mock framework is commonly used with bUnit for service mocking?**

   - a) NUnit

   - b) xUnit

   - c) Moq

   - d) Faker

Answers:

1. C
2. C
3. C

ACTIVITY: BUILD A FULL TEST SUITE FOR A REAL COMPONENT

Objective: Use bUnit to write a complete set of tests for one of your previously built interactive components.

Steps:

1. **Choose a Component:**
   Select a component from earlier chapters (e.g., *FeedbackForm*, *UserRegistrationForm*, or *ShoppingCart*).

2. **Create Test Cases:**

   o Verify initial render state

   o Simulate user interaction (e.g., button click, form entry)

   o Assert correct rendering, output, and behavior

3. **Use Mock Services (Optional):**
   If your component depends on a service, use *Moq* to create a mock implementation and inject it into the test.

4. **Validate State Changes:**
   Test how component state updates in response to actions or parameter changes.

5. **Test Error Handling (Optional):**
   Trigger an error condition (such as invalid input) and assert that the UI responds appropriately.

☑ Bonus Challenge:

- Use *OnAfterRenderAsync* in the component and write a test that validates behavior triggered during lifecycle events.

- Write a test that checks for a conditional success message after form submission.

Progressive Web Apps (PWAs) combine the best features of web and native applications. They offer users a seamless and responsive experience, even when offline. In this chapter, you'll learn how to create PWAs using Blazor WebAssembly.

What is a Progressive Web App?

A Progressive Web App is a web-based application designed to feel like a native app.

Key features of PWAs include:

- Offline support

- Installation to home screen

- Responsive and adaptive UI

- Background synchronization

Creating a Blazor WebAssembly PWA in Visual Studio

Follow these steps to create a new Blazor WebAssembly project with Progressive Web App support using Visual Studio:

1. **Open Visual Studio**

Launch Visual Studio 2022 or later.

2. **Create a New Project**

    o   Click **Create a new project**.

    o   In the "Create a new project" window, search for **Blazor WebAssembly App**.

    o   Select it and click **Next**.

3. **Configure the Project**

    o   Enter a name for your project (e.g., *MyBlazorPWA*).

    o   Choose a location and solution name.

o Click **Next**.

4. **Select Project Options**

In the "Additional information" window:

- o **Target Framework:** Choose **.NET 8.0** or **.NET 9.0**.

- o **Authentication Type:** Select **None** for now (or choose an option based on your needs).

- o **Check the box** for **Progressive Web Application**.

- o Leave **ASP.NET Core hosted** unchecked unless you are building a full-stack Blazor app with a server backend.

Click **Create**.

5. **Verify PWA Support**

Once your project is created, confirm the presence of these files in the ***wwwroot*** folder:

- o *manifest.json*

- o *service-worker.js*

- o *service-worker.published.js*

These files are essential for offline support and PWA functionality.

Customizing the Service Worker

The service worker is a JavaScript file that enables offline functionality by caching resources and intercepting requests.

To customize it:

- Open *wwwroot/service-worker.published.js*

- Modify the caching behavior as needed:

```
self.addEventListener('fetch', event => {
  event.respondWith(
    caches.match(event.request).then(response => {
```

```
      return response || fetch(event.request);
   })
  );
});
```

Offline Mode and Data Caching

To allow your app to work offline:

- Cache static assets such as HTML, CSS, and JavaScript files

- Store dynamic content locally using IndexedDB or the Cache API

Deploying a Blazor WebAssembly PWA in Visual Studio

Once your PWA is ready, you can publish and deploy it directly from Visual Studio to a static web host like **Azure Static Web Apps**, **Azure Blob Storage**, **GitHub Pages**, or another static host.

Option 1: Deploy to a Local Folder (for FTP, GitHub Pages, or Manual Upload)

1. **Right-click your project** in Solution Explorer (the Blazor WebAssembly project, not the solution).

2. Choose **Publish**.

3. Click **+ New Profile**.

4. Select **Folder** and click **Next**.

5. Choose a folder path (e.g., C:\Deployments\MyBlazorPWA) and click **Finish**.

6. Click **Publish** to generate the release version.

After publishing, your static files will be in that folder. You can now:

- Upload them to a web server via FTP.

- Push them to GitHub Pages (from a gh-pages branch).

- Upload to static storage (like S3 or Azure Blob).

Option 2: Deploy to Azure Static Web Apps

1. Right-click the project and choose **Publish**.

2. Click **+ New Profile**.

3. Select **Azure** → **Azure Static Web Apps (Preview)** and click **Next**.

4. Sign in to your Azure account if prompted.

5. Choose or create your **Static Web App** resource.

6. Configure the build and output settings if needed.

7. Click **Finish**, then **Publish**.

Visual Studio will build your project and deploy it automatically.

1. **Which file is essential for configuring PWA metadata?**

   o   a) service-worker.js

   o   b) appsettings.json

   o   c) manifest.json

   o   d) index.html

2. **Which technology helps PWAs store data locally for offline use?**

   o   a) LocalStorage

   o   b) SessionStorage

   o   c) IndexedDB

   o   d) Cookies

3. **What command creates a Blazor WebAssembly project configured as a PWA?**

   o   a) dotnet new blazorserver --pwa

   o   b) dotnet new blazorwasm --pwa

   o   c) dotnet new mvc --pwa

   o   d) dotnet new razor --pwa

Answers:

1. C
2. C
3. B

ACTIVITY: BUILD AND TEST A BLAZOR PWA WITH OFFLINE SUPPORT

Objective: Create a Progressive Web App using Blazor WebAssembly, configure offline functionality, and test it using browser developer tools.

Steps:

1. Create a new Blazor WebAssembly project with PWA support (via Visual Studio or with the *--pwa* CLI flag).

2. Customize *service-worker.published.js* to cache additional assets such as JSON files, CSS, or images.

3. Add an interactive feature, like a to-do list or a simple form, and make sure it still works when offline.

4. Deploy the project to Azure Static Web Apps or GitHub Pages.

5. Open the deployed app in Chrome or Edge, enable **Offline** mode in DevTools, and test its functionality.

☑ Bonus Challenge:

- Use IndexedDB (via *Blazored.LocalStorage* or a JavaScript wrapper) to persist user data locally.

- Add an "Install App" button that triggers the browser's PWA install prompt using *navigator.serviceWorker*.

CHAPTER 17: REAL-TIME APPLICATIONS WITH SIGNALR

Real-time functionality enables Blazor applications to push updates to users instantly without requiring a manual refresh. In this chapter, you'll learn how to implement real-time capabilities in a .NET 9 Blazor Web App using SignalR and the new interactive server component model.

What is SignalR?

SignalR is a library for ASP.NET that enables server code to push content to connected clients in real time using WebSockets or fallback transports. It's commonly used in:

- Chat applications

- Real-time dashboards

- Notifications and alerts

- Collaborative tools

Setting Up SignalR in a .NET 9 Blazor Web App

Full Example: To use SignalR with Blazor's new Web App model (in server-interactive mode), follow these steps:

Step 1: Add the SignalR Hub

Create a folder named Hubs, then add a new class called *ChatHub.cs*:

```
using Microsoft.AspNetCore.SignalR;

public class ChatHub : Hub
{
    public async Task SendMessage(string user, string message)
    {
        await Clients.All.SendAsync("ReceiveMessage", user, message);
    }
}
```

Step 2: Register SignalR in Program.cs

Update your *Program.cs* file to include *SignalR* and interactive rendering:

```
var builder = WebApplication.CreateBuilder(args);

builder.Services.AddRazorComponents().AddInteractiveServerComponents();

builder.Services.AddSignalR(); // Add SignalR support

var app = builder.Build();

app.MapRazorComponents<App>().AddInteractiveServerRenderMode();

app.MapHub<ChatHub>("/chathub"); // Map your hub endpoint

app.Run();
```

Step 3: Install the SignalR Client NuGet Package

Your component needs the *Microsoft.AspNetCore.SignalR.Client* library to use *HubConnection*.

In Visual Studio:

1. Right-click your Blazor project > **Manage NuGet Packages**

2. Go to the **Browse** tab

3. Search for *Microsoft.AspNetCore.SignalR.Client*

4. Select it and click **Install**

Step 4: Create the Chat Component

Create a component that uses SignalR in server-interactive mode.

Chat.razor

```
@inject NavigationManager Navigation
@implements IAsyncDisposable
@using Microsoft.AspNetCore.SignalR.Client

<input @bind="message" placeholder="Type a message" />
<button @onclick="SendMessage">Send</button>
```

```
<ul>
    @foreach (var msg in messages)
    {
        <li>@msg</li>
    }
</ul>

@code {
    private HubConnection? hubConnection;
    private List<string> messages = new();
    private string message = string.Empty;

    protected override async Task OnInitializedAsync()
    {
        hubConnection = new HubConnectionBuilder()
            .WithUrl(Navigation.ToAbsoluteUri("/chathub"))
            .Build();

        hubConnection.On<string, string>("ReceiveMessage", (user, msg) =>
        {
            messages.Add($"{user}: {msg}");
            InvokeAsync(StateHasChanged);
        });
        await hubConnection.StartAsync();
    }

    private async Task SendMessage()
    {
        if (!string.IsNullOrWhiteSpace(message) && hubConnection is not
null)
        {
            await hubConnection.SendAsync("SendMessage", "User", message);
            message = string.Empty;
        }
    }

    public async ValueTask DisposeAsync()
    {
        if (hubConnection is not null)
        {
            await hubConnection.DisposeAsync();
        }
    }
}
```

Step 5: Add the Component to a Page

Open your *Pages/Home.razor* or wherever you want it to appear, and add:

```
<Chat @rendermode="InteractiveServer" />
```

Step 6: Run and Test

1. Run your project.

2. Open the app in two different browser windows.

3. Type a message in one window and press **Send**.

4. You should see the message appear in **both** windows in real time.

MINI QUIZ: REAL-TIME APPLICATIONS WITH SIGNALR

1. **What is the primary purpose of SignalR in a Blazor application?**

   - o a) Improve CSS performance

   - o b) Provide real-time client-server communication

   - o c) Manage routing in components

   - o d) Store data offline

2. **Which method is used in a SignalR Hub to send a message to all connected clients?**

   - o a) SendToAll

   - o b) PushAsync

   - o c) Clients.All.SendAsync

   - o d) BroadcastMessage

3. **Which interface should a Blazor component implement to dispose of a SignalR connection cleanly?**

   - o a) IDisposable

   - o b) ICleanup

   - o c) IAsyncDisposable

   - o d) IComponentHandler

Answers:

1. B
2. C
3. C

ACTIVITY: ENHANCE YOUR CHAT APP WITH USERNAMES AND STATUS

Objective: Extend your real-time chat component by allowing users to enter their name, display connection status, and manage the message list more effectively.

Steps:

1. **Add a username field** at the top of the chat component. Prompt the user to enter a name before sending messages.

2. **Update messages** to include the username (e.g., "**Alex**: Hello!").

3. **Add a connection status badge** that shows whether the SignalR connection is active or not. Use *hubConnection.State* and refresh it on reconnect/disconnect events.

4. **Limit the visible message history** to the 10 most recent messages by trimming the list after each new message.

☑ Bonus Challenge:

- Show the connection status using color (e.g., green for connected, red for disconnected).

- Add an automatic reconnect attempt if the connection drops.

- Allow users to choose a color or emoji for their messages (optional style customization).

CHAPTER 18: ACCESSIBILITY BEST PRACTICES

Ensuring your Blazor applications are accessible makes them usable for everyone, including people with visual, auditory, cognitive, or motor disabilities. Accessibility not only improves the user experience but is often required by law in many industries.

Why Accessibility Matters

Accessibility:

- Increases usability for all users

- Broadens your app's audience

- Improves SEO and mobile performance

- Demonstrates inclusive, user-first design thinking

Key considerations include:

- Screen reader compatibility

- Keyboard-only navigation

- Sufficient color contrast

- Semantic HTML structure and ARIA support

Implementing ARIA Roles and Attributes

ARIA (Accessible Rich Internet Applications) attributes communicate intent and structure to assistive technologies:

Purpose	Example
Identifying a role	role="dialog" or role="alert"
Labeling an input	aria-label="Search field"

Purpose	Example
Describing elements	aria-describedby="descriptionId"
Live announcements	aria-live="polite"

Use ARIA to *enhance* semantic HTML, not replace it.

Keyboard Navigation

Accessible apps must work without a mouse:

- Use semantic tags like *<button>*, *<a>*, and *<input>*, which are inherently keyboard-accessible.

- Avoid clickable *<div>* or *<span>* without roles and key handlers.

- Manage focus using *@ref* and *ElementReference.FocusAsync()* in Blazor when needed.

Testing Accessibility

Test early and often using **In-browser Tools:**

- Chrome DevTools → Accessibility panel

- Firefox Accessibility Inspector

Building Accessible Components

Follow these best practices:

- Use *label* elements linked with *for* and matching *id*

- Provide instructions via *aria-describedby* or adjacent text

- Use *role="alert"* with *aria-live* for dynamic success or error messages

- Ensure contrast meets WCAG AA: Contrast Checker

- Add visual focus indicators (CSS *:focus*) for keyboard users

This example shows how to make a Blazor form accessible to screen reader users, keyboard users, and automated tools by applying semantic HTML, ARIA attributes, and validation feedback.

Step 1: Build a Semantic Feedback Form

```
@page "/feedback"
@rendermode InteractiveServer

<h3 id="formTitle">Feedback Form</h3>
<EditForm Model="@feedback" OnValidSubmit="HandleSubmit" aria-
labelledby="formTitle" role="form">
    <DataAnnotationsValidator />
    <ValidationSummary />

    <div class="form-group">
        <label for="name">Name</label>
        <InputText id="name" class="form-control" @bind-
Value="feedback.Name"
                   aria-required="true" aria-describedby="nameDesc" />
        <small id="nameDesc">Enter your full name.</small>
        <ValidationMessage For="@(() => feedback.Name)" />
    </div>

    <div class="form-group">
        <label for="comments">Comments</label>
        <InputTextArea id="comments" class="form-control" @bind-
Value="feedback.Comments"
                       aria-required="true" aria-describedby="commentsDesc"
/>
        <small id="commentsDesc">Write your message or feedback
here.</small>
        <ValidationMessage For="@(() => feedback.Comments)" />
    </div>

    <button type="submit" class="btn btn-primary">Submit</button>
</EditForm>

@if (submitted)
{
    <p class="alert alert-success" role="alert" aria-live="polite">
        Thanks for your feedback!
    </p>
}
```

Step 2: Handle Submission in Code

```
@code {
    private FeedbackModel feedback = new();
    private bool submitted = false;

    private void HandleSubmit()
    {
        submitted = true;
    }

    public class FeedbackModel
    {
        [Required]
        public string Name { get; set; }

        [Required]
        public string Comments { get; set; }
    }
}
```

MINI QUIZ: ACCESSIBILITY BEST PRACTICES

1. **Which attribute announces dynamic content changes to screen readers?**

   - a) aria-label
   - b) aria-live
   - c) aria-role
   - d) aria-hidden

2. **Which tool is commonly used to test web accessibility?**

   - a) Resharper
   - b) Lighthouse
   - c) SonarLint
   - d) Azure Monitor

3. **Why is semantic HTML important for accessibility?**

   - a) It loads faster
   - b) It helps screen readers interpret content
   - c) It improves SEO
   - d) It reduces JavaScript errors

Answers:

   1. B
   2. B
   3. B

ACTIVITY: APPLY ACCESSIBILITY ENHANCEMENTS TO A UI COMPONENT

Objective: Strengthen the accessibility of a Blazor component by applying best practices for screen readers, keyboard navigation, and dynamic feedback.

Steps:

1. Select a component you've built earlier (e.g., *ModalDialog*, *SurveyForm*, or *UserRegistrationForm*).

2. Add appropriate ARIA roles such as *role="dialog"* or *role="form"*, and attributes like *aria-label*, *aria-describedby*, or *aria-live*.

3. Ensure all *<label>* elements are correctly associated with form inputs using the *for* and *id* attributes.

4. Navigate your component using only the **Tab** key to confirm that all interactive elements are reachable and usable.

5. Run an accessibility audit using **Lighthouse** (Chrome DevTools) or **Axe** and resolve any flagged issues.

☑ Bonus Challenge:

- Use *@ref* and *ElementReference.FocusAsync()* (or JavaScript interop) to move focus to the first invalid input field after form submission.

- Add *aria-live* regions to announce real-time updates like loading indicators or confirmation messages.

CHAPTER 19: ERROR LOGGING AND MONITORING

Robust error logging and monitoring are essential for building resilient, maintainable Blazor apps. Whether you're debugging during development or tracking behavior in production, tools like *ILogger<T>* and Application Insights help you capture critical insights.

Why Logging Matters

Logging allows you to:

- Trace application behavior and user interactions

- Diagnose bugs and performance issues

- Capture exceptions and failures

- Monitor usage in production

Log Levels

.NET provides several log levels:

- **Trace** – Detailed information for diagnosing problems

- **Debug** – Used for debugging during development

- **Information** – Key events in the application lifecycle

- **Warning** – Unexpected or unusual behavior that doesn't stop execution

- **Error** – An issue that caused a specific operation to fail

- **Critical** – A failure that requires immediate attention

Using *ILogger* in Blazor Components

Inject the logger directly into components or services.

In a Razor Component:

```
@inject ILogger<WeatherComponent> Logger
```

```
<h3>Weather Dashboard</h3>

@code {
    protected override void OnInitialized()
    {
        Logger.LogInformation("WeatherComponent initialized at {Time}",
DateTime.Now);
    }
}
```

In a service class:

```
public class DataService
{
    private readonly ILogger<DataService> _logger;

    public DataService(ILogger<DataService> logger)
    {
        _logger = logger;
    }

    public void LoadData()
    {
        _logger.LogDebug("Loading data at {Time}", DateTime.UtcNow);
    }

    public void SimulateError()
    {
        try
        {
            throw new InvalidOperationException("Data failed to load");
        }
        catch (Exception ex)
        {
            _logger.LogError(ex, "An error occurred while loading data");
        }
    }
}
```

Configure Logging Output

In *appsettings.json*:

```
"Logging": {
  "LogLevel": {
    "Default": "Information",
    "Microsoft": "Warning",
    "Microsoft.Hosting.Lifetime": "Information"
  }
}
```

This controls which logs are captured by default and suppresses excessive internal framework noise.

Integrating Application Insights with Visual Studio

Application Insights is a telemetry service that helps you detect and diagnose issues in real time.

Here's how to integrate it using Visual Studio:

1. Add Application Insights via Visual Studio

- Right-click your project in **Solution Explorer**.

- Choose **Add** > **Connected Service**.

- Select **Application Insights**.

- Follow the prompts to connect your app to an existing Azure Application Insights resource, or create a new one.

Visual Studio will automatically:

- Add the required NuGet package.

- Register Application Insights in *Program.cs*.

- Insert your Instrumentation Key or Connection String in *appsettings.json*.

2. What Gets Tracked Automatically

- Page views

- Unhandled exceptions

- Dependency calls (e.g., HTTP or SQL)

- Custom events and metrics (you can add your own)

Custom Events and Exception Tracking

You can log custom events and track exceptions explicitly.

Tracking Custom Events

```
@inject TelemetryClient Telemetry

Telemetry.TrackEvent("UserSignedIn");
```

Capturing Exceptions

```
try {
    // risky logic
} catch (Exception ex) {
    Logger.LogError(ex, "Unexpected error occurred");
}
```

This example demonstrates structured logging in both a Blazor component and a service class, and how to send that telemetry to Application Insights for real-time monitoring.

Step 1: Log from a Component

```
@inject ILogger<WeatherComponent> Logger

<h3>Weather Dashboard</h3>

@code {
    protected override void OnInitialized()
    {
        Logger.LogInformation("WeatherComponent initialized at {Time}",
DateTime.Now);
    }
}
```

This logs an informational message to the default logging provider.

Step 2: Add Logging to a Service

```
public class DataService
{
    private readonly ILogger<DataService> _logger;

    public DataService(ILogger<DataService> logger)
    {
        _logger = logger;
    }

    public void LoadData()
    {
        _logger.LogDebug("Loading data at {Time}", DateTime.UtcNow);
    }

    public void SimulateError()
    {
        try
        {
            throw new InvalidOperationException("Data failed to load");
        }
```

```
        catch (Exception ex)
        {
            _logger.LogError(ex, "An error occurred while loading data");
        }
    }
}
```

Step 3: Configure Logging in *appsettings.json*:

```
"Logging": {
  "LogLevel": {
    "Default": "Information",
    "Microsoft": "Warning"
  }
}
```

Step 4: Add Application Insights via Visual Studio

- Right-click the project > **Add** > **Connected Service**

- Choose **Application Insights** and follow the prompts

- Confirm the following are updated:

    o **NuGet Package**: *Microsoft.ApplicationInsights.AspNetCore*

    o ***Program.cs***:

```
builder.Services.AddApplicationInsightsTelemetry();
```

    o **appsettings.json**:

```
"ApplicationInsights": {
  "ConnectionString": "InstrumentationKey=..."
}
```

Now, logs, events, and telemetry will flow to your Application Insights dashboard in Azure.

MINI QUIZ: ERROR LOGGING AND MONITORING

1. **What class is used for structured logging in Blazor?**

    o   a) LogManager

    o   b) ITracer

    o   c) ILogger

    o   d) TraceWriter

2. **Where can Application Insights be configured in a Blazor app?**

    o   a) Only in the cloud portal

    o   b) In appsettings.json or Program.cs

    o   c) Through Razor syntax

    o   d) It can't be configured manually

3. **What log level should be used for catching critical errors in production?**

    o   a) Debug

    o   b) Information

    o   c) Warning

    o   d) Error or Critical

Answers:

1. C
2. B
3. D

ACTIVITY: ADD LOGGING AND MONITORING

Objective: Integrate structured logging and real-time monitoring into your Blazor app to enhance observability and maintainability.

Steps:

1. Select a component or service that performs data loading, form handling, or user interactions.

2. Inject *ILogger<T>* and add log statements for the following levels:

    o   *Information* (e.g., component loaded or user action triggered)

    o   *Warning* (e.g., unusual but non-breaking behavior)

    o   *Error* (e.g., when an operation fails)

3. Simulate an exception in a *try/catch* block and log it using *LogError*.

4. Add Application Insights via Visual Studio and verify that logs appear in the Azure portal.

☑ Bonus Challenge:

• Set up a custom logging provider that writes logs to a local file or external system.
• Use Application Insights Analytics to:

  •   Visualize request/exception trends

  •   Trigger alerts when error rates spike

Robust deployment and hosting practices allow your Blazor applications to reach users reliably and efficiently. This chapter introduces you to multiple hosting options, deployment workflows, and CI/CD integration.

Why Deployment Matters

You'll learn to:

- Choose the right hosting model for your app

- Deploy using Visual Studio or GitHub

- Automate deployment using CI/CD pipelines

Choosing the Right Hosting Option

Blazor apps can be hosted in several ways. Here's a quick guide to which model fits which use case:

- **Blazor Server** – Best for real-time, interactive apps with server-side processing

- **Blazor WebAssembly (WASM)** – Best for lightweight static sites and Progressive Web Apps (PWAs)

- **Blazor Hybrid** – Best for native desktop and mobile apps built using .NET MAUI

Deploying Blazor Server Apps to Azure

Azure provides straightforward hosting solutions for Blazor Server applications.

Deploying Blazor Server Apps to Azure App Service

Azure App Service makes it easy to deploy and host Blazor Server applications.

Step-by-Step Deployment Using Visual Studio

1. **Publish Your App**

- o In Solution Explorer, right-click the **Blazor Server** project

- o Select **Publish**

- o Choose **Azure** > **Azure App Service (Windows/Linux)**

- o Click **Next** and either create a new App Service or select an existing one

2. **Configure the App Service**

- o Choose a unique name for your app

- o Select your desired region, service plan, and runtime (.NET 9.0)

- o Click **Finish**, then **Publish**

Once published, your app will be live and accessible via the Azure-provided URL.

Deploying Blazor WebAssembly Apps to Azure Static Web Apps

Blazor WASM apps are static and ideal for Azure Static Web Apps, which automatically handle hosting, SSL, and global CDN distribution.

Step-by-Step Deployment Using Visual Studio

1. **Publish Your App Locally**

- o In Solution Explorer, right-click your **Blazor WebAssembly** project

- o Choose **Publish**

- o Select **Folder**, then click **Next**

- o Choose a folder location and click **Finish**

- o Click **Publish** to generate the production build

2. **Upload to Azure Static Web Apps**

- o In the Azure Portal, create a new **Static Web App**

- o Upload the published *wwwroot* folder

- o Azure will host your static content and provide a public URL

MINI QUIZ: DEPLOYMENT AND HOSTING

1. **Which Azure hosting service is ideal for Blazor WebAssembly?**

    o   A) Azure VM

    o   B) Azure Static Web Apps

    o   C) Azure SQL Database

    o   D) Azure Container Instances

2. **What file automates CI/CD workflows in GitHub?**

    o   A) .gitignore

    o   B) appsettings.json

    o   C) .github/workflows/deploy.yml

    o   D) deploy.config

3. **Which hosting option supports deploying Blazor apps as native applications?**

    o   A) Blazor WebAssembly

    o   B) Blazor Server

    o   C) Blazor Hybrid (MAUI)

    o   D) Azure Static Web Apps

Answers:

1. B
2. C
3. C

ACTIVITY: DEPLOY YOUR FIRST BLAZOR APP TO AZURE

Objective: Practice deploying a Blazor WebAssembly project to Azure Static Web Apps.

Steps:

1. Create a new Blazor WebAssembly app in Visual Studio.

2. Initialize a Git repository and push the code to GitHub.

3. Go to the Azure Portal and create a new Static Web App.

4. Link your GitHub repo and let Azure deploy the app.

5. Visit the generated site URL to confirm it works.

☑ Bonus Challenge:

- Customize the homepage or add a new page before redeploying.

- Use the Azure portal to view build logs and monitor deployments.

Next Steps in Your Blazor Journey

Congratulations! By completing this book, you've taken a significant step toward mastering Blazor and building powerful web applications using .NET. But your journey doesn't stop here.

Here's how you can continue growing:

- **Build a real-world project** – Apply what you've learned by building something useful — a dashboard, a blog platform, or a scheduling tool. Focus on solving a real problem to stay motivated and reinforce your skills.
- **Explore official documentation** – Microsoft's Blazor docs continue to expand and are full of practical examples and advanced use cases.
- **Join the community** – Engage in forums like Stack Overflow, GitHub, Reddit, or the .NET Discord to ask questions, help others, and stay inspired.
- **Stay updated** – With .NET and Blazor evolving rapidly, keep an eye on release notes, conference talks, and community blogs.
- **Contribute** – Once you're confident, share your knowledge — write tutorials, give talks, or contribute to open-source projects.

Resources for Continued Learning

Here are some recommended resources to continue your learning:

- Microsoft Learn – https://learn.microsoft.com/en-us/training/
- unQbd – Offers affordable streaming access to Blazor books and tutorials (https://unQbd.com)
- ASP.NET Community Standups – https://live.asp.net/
- GitHub – Explore repositories from open-source Blazor projects

Encouragement

You've learned how to structure components, handle user input, manage state, and deploy applications using C# and Blazor. Whether you go on to build enterprise tools, indie projects, or teach others, know that you're part of a growing and vibrant developer community.

Keep building. Keep learning. Keep going.

Happy coding, and welcome to the Blazor community!

Adam Seebeck